Coaching the Special Teams:
The Winning Edge in Football

Coaching the Special Teams: The Winning Edge in Football

Tom Simonton

Parker Publishing Company, Inc.
West Nyack, N.Y.

Library of Congress Cataloging in Publication Data

Simonton, Tom,
    Coaching the special teams.

    Includes index.
    1. Football coaching. I. Title.
GV954.4.S57   796.33'2077   77-2613
ISBN 0-13-139253-0

Printed in the United States of America

Dedicated to the Dublin High School coaching staff—

Travis Davis
Doug Metts
Richard Johnson
Kenny Webb
Alan Yauck
Ernest Wade
Taylor Lovell

How This Book
Can Strengthen Your Team

There are three things any football team must have to win consistently: (1) an *offense* that can move the football, (2) a *defense* that can stop the opposition, and, equally important, (3) *special teams* that can effectively perform specialized assignments. These assignments range from opening game kickoffs to the end of game two-minute offense. A deficiency in any of these three areas can mean defeat. This book examines in detail all aspects of the third category, the special teams.

While preparing this material I became more aware of the great number of techniques that must be taught and skills that must be developed, in order to have sound special teams. The value of this book is that it can serve as a reference book for every type of special team. It is not limited by one idea or plan for each special team. Instead, a variety of diagrams illustrate many different ideas and allow the coach to alter or change his special team pattern not only from season to season but also from game to game. The book is an invaluable on-the-field guide and teaching manual containing 165 diagrams that clearly show every phase of special team operation.

One of the greatest problems of developing special teams is the limited practice time available to most squads. Chapter One deals with this problem. It includes a detailed, day-by-day practice schedule showing how each special team can be coached without cutting deeply into the regular offensive and defensive practice time.

Every type of special team is covered:
— the kickoff and kickoff receiving teams
— the punting team and the punt receiving team
— the extra point team and the extra point defense team
— the field goal team and the quick-kick team
— the onside kick team and the onside kick receiving team
— the goal line offense and the goal line defense teams
— the pass defense and rushing defense teams
— the prevent defense and the two-minute offense teams

There is no easy way to success. The teams that excel are those that are willing to work hard perfecting the details of every phase of the game, including special teams. Use the material in this book year after year. Change styles and patterns of the special teams to keep opponents from learning your game plan. And above all else, sell your players on the idea that *special teams can and will win games!*

Tom Simonton

Table of Contents

6. THE EXTRA POINT SPECIAL TEAM 78

7. THE EXTRA POINT DEFENSE SPECIAL TEAM 87

8. THE FIELD GOAL SPECIAL TEAM 92

9. THE ONSIDE KICK SPECIAL TEAM 99

12.   THE GOAL LINE STAND SPECIAL TEAM *(Cont.)*

13.   THE GOAL LINE OFFENSE SPECIAL TEAM   140

14.   THE PASS DEFENSE SPECIAL TEAM   163

Coaching the Special Teams:
The Winning Edge in Football

1

Planning for the Special Teams

A "special team" is any group of offensive or defensive players, all possessing certain skills or talents, who are inserted into the game at a particular time in order to perform a specialized job. Once the special team has completed its assignment it is removed from the game.

WHO IS ASSIGNED TO SPECIAL TEAMS?

Any player on the squad may be a special team member. It could be a regular offensive or defensive starter who desires to play 48 minutes and can physically do it. Or it could be a non-regular member of the team who possesses a particular talent needed only on a special team.

REQUIREMENTS OF SPECIAL TEAM MEMBERS

The main requirements are *spirit* and *enthusiasm*. There are always some team members who do not like special team assignments. These players are probably offensive or defensive starters who are seeing plenty of action and feel they need to rest at certain times, such as during kicking situations. For this reason these players would probably not have the spirit and enthusiasm necessary for special team assignments. Although spirit and enthusiasm are top requirements, many special team players will also need a special skill. Examples of these players are punters, snappers, kick-off men, extra point holders and kickers, pass defenders, etc. Above all, select those players who love to play and who will take pride in their special team.

MORALE OF SPECIAL TEAM MEMBERS

The coach must make every effort to convince his players of the importance of special teams. He must make each member feel, and rightly so, that he is contributing just as much to the success of the team as the regular offensive or defensive starter.

A good start would be to arrange with the local radio and newspaper sports directors to give special teams particular notice in their pre-game and post-game stories. Before the season starts the coach should invite all members of the local press to a meeting where the purpose of the special teams is reviewed. The press should be told when and how each special team is to be used. Names and photos (if possible) of all special team members should be made available to the press. A chart diagramming where each special team player will be positioned would be of great value to the media. The coach should encourage writers and broadcasters to give as much publicity as possible to each member, and to take special notice of how they contribute to each win.

Since all players like to be known around their own school, the coach can give the special team members prestige by having the cheerleaders make signs and posters drawing attention to special team members and their contributions to the team. (See Figure 1-1 for an example.)

The presence of special teams greatly improves squad morale. Morale is developed during enthusiastic practices where all team members have an opportunity to contribute. A variety of special teams provides ample opportunity for a large number of players to consider themselves "starters."

SPECIAL AWARDS AND INCENTIVES
FOR SPECIAL TEAM PLAYERS

The morale of special team players can be boosted by awards during the season as well as at the end-of-season banquet. Small

DUBLIN IRISH EXTRA POINT TEAM
Kicked 5 extra points in 5 attempts last Friday
in 35-7 victory over   High

Ends—Blan Trollinger	☐	Don Edwards	☐
Tackles—Matt Roberts	☐	Bill Larsen	☐
Guards—Stan Stanley	☐	Bill Pollard	☐
Center—Stan Couey	☐		
Backs—Eddie Dudley	☐	Jimmy Williams	☐
Holder—Steve Edwards	☐	Kicker—Pat Hodges	☐

Team has not missed an extra point this season!

(Note to Coach: Place small photo of each player in box beside player's
name.)

FIGURE 1-1

helmet decals are one of the best awards for special team players.
These decals are relatively inexpensive, even when custom made,
and can be used for identifying each special team. (Note: When
choosing special team helmet decals, be careful not to ruin the
overall team look of the helmet. Special team decals should be
small.)

Figure 1-2 shows some examples of special team decals. Each
coach should try to design unique decals relating to his team's
nickname or mascot. **Example:** A school with the nickname *Indians*
could use an arrowhead decal to identify members of the extra
point team, a tomahawk decal for members of the kickoff team, etc.
The decals can be quickly and easily applied, or taken off, at a
moment's notice as special team members change due to injury or
other causes.

At the end-of-season banquet special team members should be
recognized and highlights of their season recounted. The coach
might want to gather statistics to show how the special teams con-
tributed to the winning season. He might announce at the banquet

EXAMPLES OF SPECIAL TEAM HELMET DECALS

FIGURE 1-2

that two of the ten games were won by extra points (shedding glory on the entire extra point team), or that the special goal line stand team allowed only one touchdown during the 31 plays they were on the field. Special cloth emblems, similar to helmet decals, could be awarded to all special team players and these could be sewn on award jackets or sweaters. Small trophies or plaques could be awarded for outstanding achievement by special team members if the coach desires.

SPECIAL TEAM CAPTAINS

Captains (not to be confused with regular team captains) should be selected for each special team. The captain's job would be to act as a go-between between the coach and the special team players. He would be responsible for keeping his unit together and ready to enter the game at the proper time. **Example:** During a game the captain of the special punting team should begin to call together his team members after the second down if it appears a first down will be difficult to make. The players are then ready to enter the game quickly if the third-down play does not make the necessary first-down yardage. Each special team captain must keep himself aware of injuries to his players and be sure the coach has a replacement ready.

SPECIAL TEAMS PLAYER ASSIGNMENT CHART

Since there will probably be a wide assortment of players assigned to special teams, the coach may find it beneficial to keep a "Special Teams Players Assignment Chart." This chart would be useful at practice as well as at games. Figure 1-3 shows such a

SPECIAL TEAMS PLAYER ASSIGNMENT CHART

KICKOFF RECEIVING TEAM

	Bobby McCann	Stan Stanley	Stan Couey	Bill Larsen	Matt Roberts	
Don Edwards						Blan Trollinger
		Andy Ullrich		Stewart McElwaney		
	Kenny Hall			Robert Haygood		

Substitutes: Front line (Wallace, Holcombe)   Ends (Tenny)
        Backs (Ayers)

GOAL LINE DEFENSE TEAM

Henry Asberry	Mike Wallace	Stan Stanley	James Simon	Wayne Holcombe	Blan Trollinger
	Andy Ullrich		Stewart McElwaney		
Robert Haygood		Steve Edwards		Bobby Sumlin	

Substitutes: Linemen (Larsen, Burke)   Linebackers (Dudley)
        Backs (Williams)

TWO-MINUTE OFFENSE TEAM

Don Edwards	Bobby McCann	Alan Crabb	Jim Moran	Bill Pollard	Jerry Jobe	Greg Rooks
			Steve Edwards			Warren Burnette
		Robert Haygood		Stewart McElwaney		

FIGURE 1-3

chart. (**Note:** *All* special teams should be listed on the chart although we are listing only a few as an example.) Be sure the chart includes names of substitutes for each special team.

PRACTICING THE SPECIAL TEAMS

Each special team's strength will be in direct proportion to the amount of practice time allotted to it. No coach should expect a kickoff return team or a two-minute offense special team to perform well if they are drilled only a few times during the season. All practices should provide some time for individual coaching of special team players. A chart such as the one in Figure 1-4 would allow the coach to keep an accurate record of how much time is provided for special team instruction.

TEAM	Mon Oct. 1	Tues Oct. 2	Wed Oct. 3	Thurs Oct. 4	Fri Oct. 5
Kickoff team	10 min.	10 min.		10 min.	GAME
Kickoff return team	10 min	10 min.		10 min.	,,
Punting team	10 min.	10 min.		10 min.	,,
Punt receiving team	10 min.	10 min.		10 min.	,,
Extra point team	10 min.	10 min.		10 min.	,,
Extra point defense				10 min.	,,
Onside kick team	10 min.		10 min.	5 min.	,,
Onside kick defense			10 min.	5 min.	,,
Field goal team	10 min.			5 min.	,,
Quick-kick team	10 min.		5 min.	5 min.	,,
Goal line stand defense	10 min.		5 min.	5 min.	,,
Pass defense team		20 min.	5 min.	5 min.	,,
Rushing defense team		10 min.	5 min.	5 min.	,,
Prevent defense team	5 min.		5 min.	5 min.	,,
Goal line offense team	10 min.		10 min.	10 min.	,,
Two-minute offense team	10 min.	10 min.	5 min.	5 min.	,,

FIGURE 1-4

Following is a weekly practice plan that illustrates how careful planning can provide ample practice time for all special teams. The schedule is for one week during the season leading up to a Friday night game. Practice time with special teams is indicated by italics.

MONDAY

5 minutes — Exercise
25 minutes — Offensive Group Work: backs and linemen work in separate groups.
20 minutes — Defensive Group Work: linemen, linebackers, and halfbacks work in separate groups.
Break
40 minutes — Team Offense:
     20 min. . .regular offense.
     10 min. . .goal line offense special team.
     10 min. . .two-minute offense special team.
35 minutes — Team Defense:
     20 min. . .regular defense.
     10 min. . .goal line stand special team.
     5 min. . .prevent defense special team.
10 minutes — Kicking:
     Kickoff man practices kickoffs.
     Kickoff return backs catch kickoffs.
     Snappers and punters work on punting.
     Punt receivers catch punts.
     Snappers, holders and extra point kickers work on extra points.
     Onside kickers work on onside kicks.
     Quick-kickers work on quick kicks.
     Snappers, holders and field goal kickers work on field goals.
Sprints and conditioning

TUESDAY

5 minutes — Exercise.
20 minutes — Offensive Group Work.
20 minutes — Defensive Group Work:
     All linebackers and halfbacks (including all special team pass defenders) work on pass defense.
     All linemen (including special team pass defense linemen) work on rushing the passer and playing the screen and draw.

Break

30 minutes — Team Offense:

        20 min. . .regular offense.

        10 min. . .*two-minute offense special team.*

30 minutes — Team Defense:

        20 min. . .regular defense.

        10 min. . .*rushing defense special team.*

20 minutes — Kicking:

        10 min. . .*Kickoff special team work on kicking to kickoff return special team.*

        (Use substitutes for players who are on both of these teams.)

        10 min. . .*Punt special team kicks to punt-return special team.*

        Extra point snapper, holder, kicker work on extra points at end of field.

Sprints and conditioning

WEDNESDAY

  5 minutes — Exercise.

15 minutes — Offensive Group Work.

15 minutes — Defensive Group Work.

40 minutes — Team Offense:

        20 min. . .regular offense.

        10 min. . .*goal line offense special team.*

        5 min. . .*quick-kick special team.*

        5 min. . .*two-minute offense special team.*

Break

40 minutes — Team Defense:

        20 min. . .regular defense.

        5 min. . .*goal line defense special team.*

        5 min. . .*rushing defense special team.*

        5 min. . .*pass defense special team.*

        5 min. . .*prevent defense special team.*

10 minutes — Kicking:

        10 min. . .*Onside kick special team kick to onside kick-receiving team.*

        Extra point special team kick vs. extra point defense special team.

Sprints and conditioning

THURSDAY

PRACTICE IN SHORTS
45 minutes — Kicking:

   10 min. . . *Kickoff special team kick to kickoff return special team.*

   10 min. . . *Punt special team punt to punt-receiving special team.*

   5 min. . . *Quick kick special team.*

   10 min. . . *Extra point special team against extra point defense special team.*

   5 min. . . *Field goal special team.*

   5 min. . . *Onside kick special team kick to onside kick-receiving special team.*

30 minutes — Team Defense:

   10 min. . . Review regular defense.

   5 min. . . *Review goal line defense special team.*

   5 min. . . *Review rushing defense special team.*

   5 min. . . *Review passing defense special team.*

   5 min. . . *Review prevent defense special team.*

30 minutes — Team Offense:

   15 min. . . Review regular offense.

   10 min. . . *Review goal line offense special team.*

   5 min. . . *Review two-minute offense special team.*

The coach should make sure each special team is practiced in proportion to how often it is used. **Example:** The kickoff and extra point special teams will need more work than the onside kick special team. The weekly practice schedule should be altered according to the style of the weekly opponent. **Example:** If this week's opponent runs 95% of the time and passes only as a last resort, the rushing defense special team would get more work than the passing defense special team.

As the coach makes up his weekly practice schedule he should not be too alarmed to find that only 20 minutes or so is provided for some special teams. He should remember that some special teams can get in a lot of practice in that limited time. **Examples:** The extra point special team should be able to kick 15-20 extra points in a 10-minute period and the kickoff team should be able to kickoff 5-7 times in a 10-minute period.

2

The Kickoff Special Team

SELECTING KICKOFF TEAM MEMBERS

The main requirement of a member of the kickoff team is the ability and willingness to make open field tackles. Some coaches refer to the kickoff team as "the suicide squad," due to the wide-open, full-speed style of play it requires. Open field tackling demands body control and balance in order to tackle a fast back who is running at full speed. It also requires a special toughness not found in every player Look for the following qualities in kickoff team members:

1. **Movement and Balance**. Most kickoff return men will be darting in all directions and usually will possess good speed. The tackler must be ready for fakes and stop-and-go action by the ball carrier.

2. **Tackling Ability**. Just getting into position to tackle isn't enough. The kickoff defender must be a good tackler. Arm tackling will seldom stop a running back who has had plenty of time to gather a full head of steam. Kickoff team members must be given plenty of practice in tackling a rapidly moving target. (**Drill**: Line up kickoff team members in one line as shown in Figure 2-1. Place a fast back, holding a small air dummy, on the 10-yard line. On the signal the back runs full speed up the field, holding the dummy instead of a football. The kickoff team defender sprints towards the back and makes contact with the back who is using the dummy as a shield

26

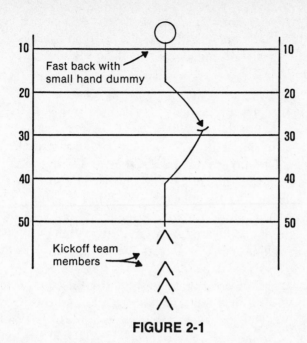

FIGURE 2-1

against injury. The defender does not tackle the back. This drill can be done live, without the dummy, if the coach desires.)

3. Speed. Speed on the kickoff team is very important but should not take priority over tackling ability. The faster the defenders can get to the ball carrier the less return yardage he will have. By all means never allow big, slow players to be used on the kickoff team!

4. Determination. This could well be the most important quality of all. No player, regardless of his abilities, will perform well if he lacks the desire to get the job done. Body size should seldom be a factor in selecting players for the kickoff team. If fact, the kickoff team is the perfect place to play the 130-150 pound players who are considered too small to play on the regular defensive team.

One final word of warning concerning selection of kickoff team members. *Do not place on the kickoff team any player who does not really want to be on it*. A half-hearted effort by a player who does not really sense the importance of the kickoff team could prove very costly. Reward kickoff team members with special helmet decals and be sure they receive good press notices when they do well. Give them game-by-game and seasonal goals to strive for. Make sure other team members recognize their value to the success of the team.

PERFECTING THE KICKER

The coach cannot always count on having a naturally talented kickoff man. Often one must be developed. During the writing of this book I started the season without a talented kicker. By the season's end we had five players who could give us a consistent kickoff. This was not due to any coaching on our part other than supplying the balls, kicking tees, and advice on the basic fundamentals of kicking off. The players, with diligent work and practice, did the rest.

During early season practice, try everyone on the team as a potential kickoff man. Line them all up and make them kick a few. Some players will lack the confidence to try unless the coach makes them. Look for the naturally strong leg, one that can power the football deep. Look also for the players who consistently get good height on their kicks. Once the coach has narrowed the potential kickers down to the top four or five, he should give them kicking tees and plenty of footballs so that they can practice on their own during their free time. One of the good points about the kicking game is that a kicker can practice his specialty by himself. The kickers should be given pointers about positioning the football on the tee properly, where to strike the football in order to get the maximum height and distance, and above all, how to work out the proper approach steps before kicking the ball. Some kickers like to approach the football from a long distance of 10-12 yards, while others prefer a 4-5 yard approach. Each kicker has his own style, but the coach should temper the style with sound kicking fundamentals such as keeping the eyes on the ball during the approach, maintaining a good follow-through, and making toe contact with the ball at the proper spot.

Once the kicker is familiar with the fundamentals the coach must encourage him to practice often. There is usually ample practice time before and/or after practice, even if the kickoff is not part of the regular practice plan.

TYPES OF KICKOFF COVERAGE

The kickoff coverage, just like a good offense or defense, must be well planned. The simplest coverage is shown in Figure 2-2. The football is resting on the 40-yard line and all members of the kickoff team are on the 35-yard line—except the kicker, whose position is determined by the number of approach steps he takes.

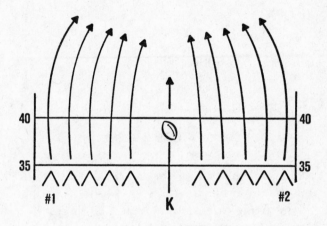

FIGURE 2-2

(**Note**: Some coaches will prefer to have the players other than the kicker in a three-point stance facing downfield. Other coaches want their players in a two-point stance, hands on their knees, facing in towards the football.) As the kicker passes the 35-yard line and approaches the football all other players begin their sprint downfield. Each player, in this type of coverage, sprints straight downfield full speed. The two outside men (labeled #1 and #2 in Figure 2-2) are given the responsibility of turning any wide return back towards the middle of the field. They must never head towards the middle of the field themselves and allow the ball carrier to get outside. They must be coached not to get deeper downfield than the ball carrier and end up chasing the ball carrier from behind (see Figure 2-3).

If the ball is returned up the middle, the two players with outside coverage responsibility should close in cautiously from the

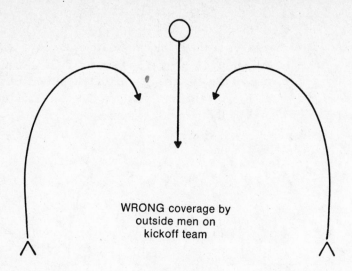

WRONG coverage by
outside men on
kickoff team

FIGURE 2-3

outside, making sure the ball carrier doesn't get outside them. All
other players should locate the direction of the football and continue downfield, being careful to "stay in their lanes." If a player
has to get out of his lane to avoid a block he should do so, but
should return to his lane after passing the blocker. Unless he does
return to his lane a hole will be created in the coverage, enabling a
good runner to get good return yardage or perhaps even a touchdown. As the defenders get near the ball carrier they should slow
down and bring themselves under control. This is to make sure
they make solid contact with the ball carrier. (If the defenders are
going full speed there is the possibility that a quick fake by the
runner will cause them to miss contact with the runner entirely.)

> *Coaching point:* In any type of kickoff coverage one player
> should be designated as a safety man. This player should be
> the last man downfield and should always keep himself be-
> tween the ball carrier and the goal line.

Figure 2-4 shows a coverage similar to the one in Figure 2-2.
The only change is that the two outside men on either side have
swapped assignments. The outside defenders sprint directly towards the ball carrier while the second men from the inside be-

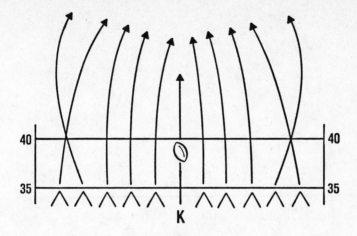

FIGURE 2-4

come contain men. All other players go for the runner in their lanes.

Some kickoff *return* teams set up their blocking plans by assigning each blocker a man according to where the man is located on the kickoff team. For example, one blocker is to block the "first man to the right of the football" or "the second widest man on the left side." When kicking off to a team who uses this style of return blocking, use a kickoff pattern similar to the one shown in Figure 2-5. The blocking pattern of the receiving team can be greatly disrupted by letting the defenders cross lanes as they cover. Be sure one defender remains back as a safety man.

Some coaches prefer the *wave* type of coverage, as shown in Figure 2-6. The first wave consists of four or five of the kickoff team's fastest players. Their job is to locate the football and head directly for the ball carrier. They do not worry about staying in lanes, but should make sure they do not follow directly behind another player as they sprint down the field.

The second wave of players should be from five to eight yards behind the first wave. They should cover by filling in the gaps between the first wave players. The job of the second wave players is to make the tackle if the first wave is not successful. The second wave will often find that many of the blockers have gone after the

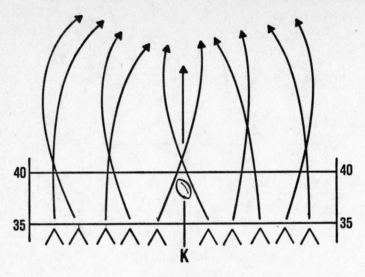

FIGURE 2-5

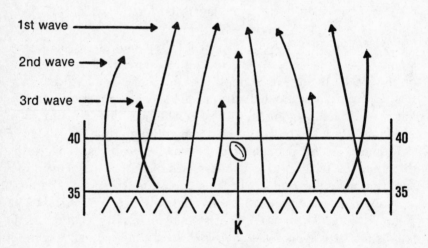

FIGURE 2-6

first wave of defenders and their path to the ball carrier will be relatively clear.

The third and last wave of defenders must include two or three of the kickoff team's best and surest tacklers. They will follow behind the second wave of defenders, keeping themselves at all times between the ball carrier and the goal line.

If the kickoff team has a kicker who can get excellent height and distance on his kicks, they may choose to kick off at an angle as shown in Figure 2-7. The football is kicked from the hash mark and angled towards the opposite corner of the field. The four fastest defenders are lined up at the opposite side of the kickoff formation. Their job is to sprint downfield as fast as possible in the direction of the angled kick. A kickoff with good height should give the fast defenders more time to get in the area of the kickoff receiver.

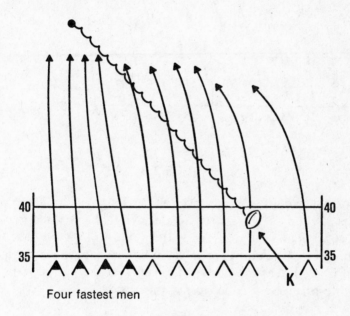

Four fastest men

FIGURE 2-7

Occasionally the kickoff team faces an opponent who is especially noted for long kickoff returns. When this occurs, the kickoff team should kick as near as possible to a designated spot where a long return is unlikely to originate. In Figure 2-8 the kickoff team is kicking to a team that has done an outstanding job setting up returns to their left side (our right side). By kicking a medium length kick and forcing their end to handle the football we have not allowed their fast deep backs to handle the ball, and we have not given the receiving team time to set up a return wall. When this type of kick is to be used, the members of the kickoff team must be

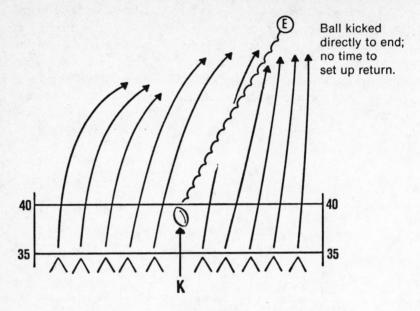

FIGURE 2-8

told so they can alter their downfield coverage in the direction of the kick. Of course, the shortened kickoff might give the opponents fairly good field position, but at the same time it probably will prevent the long return for a possible touchdown. This type of kickoff is good near the end of the half or at the end of the game when the coach prefers not to use the onside kick.

REVERSES AND TRICK PLAYS

One player must be responsible for covering each sideline on any type of kickoff the coach chooses to use. The first responsibility of these two players is to see if the ball carrier comes their way as soon as he catches the football. If he does, they must be ready to make the tackle or turn the play back to the inside. The second responsibility of these men is to watch for a reverse or trick play coming their way. The first rule in preparing for the reverse or trick play is this: *Never leave your sideline area until you are absolutely certain there is no possibility of a reverse.* When the defender is positive there is no reverse he is to angle in towards the ball carrier, maintaining his outside position.

Be sure that the players chosen for the outside containment are smart and dependable. They must accept coaching well. They must not be so eager to make a tackle that they leave their area too soon. One mistake on their part will often result in a touchdown. Figure 2-9 shows the correct contain position for the player assigned to watch for the reverse.

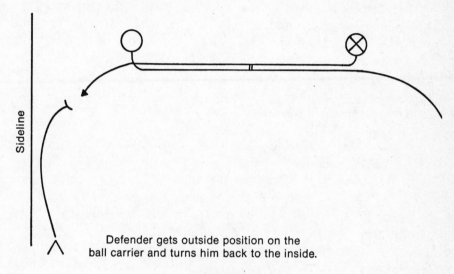

Defender gets outside position on the ball carrier and turns him back to the inside.

FIGURE 2-9

CONDITIONING THE KICKOFF TEAM

Any kickoff team that covers the kickoff slowly is allowing greater return yardage. Kickoff team members must be drilled to sprint downfield full speed. They can't do this unless they are in excellent condition. The normal daily football practice, including sprints at the end of practice, should get the kickoff team members in good shape. However, if the coach feels that extra conditioning is necessary at the end of practice, he should make it a learning situation as well as a conditioning period. Rather than just running more sprints, line up the kickoff team; as the kicker kicks the football the coach can work with individuals on staying in their lanes, watching for the reverse, coming under control before making the tackle, etc.

COACHING POINTS

Here is a list of coaching points for the kickoff team that should be thoroughly taught by the coach and understood by each kickoff team member:

1. Don't overrun the kickoff. Watch how deep the ball is kicked. Stay "in front" of the ball carrier at all times. Never get in the position of having to chase the ball carrier from behind.

2. Slow down and come under control before making the tackle. It is better to allow the ball carrier an extra yard or two than to miss making the tackle at all. Tackle with the head in front of the runner, especially when making the tackle at an angle.

3. As a general rule, tackle above the belt. Going for the ankles or knees in open field often allows a quick-stepping back to get away.

4. Use gang tackling until the whistle blows. Make sure the ball carrier is down.

5. Stay in your lane as you cover. Dodging blockers opens lanes. If you must get out of your lane swing back into it once you are past the blocker. (**Note**: Staying in lanes must be stressed by the coach. Players won't do it naturally.)

6. Whatever type of kickoff coverage is used, make sure at least one player is assigned the job of safety man. He must be fast and a sure, dependable tackler.

7. Most kickoff return teams assign one man to block the kicker as soon as he has kicked the football. The kicker must not let the fact that he will be hit very soon after kicking the ball affect his kicking style or his follow-through.

8. Some blockers make the mistake of blocking too early. If knocked down, members of the kickoff team should be prepared to get up and go again in pursuit of the ball carrier.

9. Stress the importance of not piling on after the tackle. This will only add a 15-yard penalty to the return yardage of the receiving team.

10. No kickoff team member can afford to slow down his coverage if the football is kicked to the opposite side of the field. Continue to sprint full speed, taking the proper angle of pursuit.

11. Recover any loose football after it has gone ten yards. Occasionally, a member of the kickoff receiving team will not touch

the football, hoping it will go out-of-bounds or roll into the end zone. Remember: A kickoff is a free ball after it goes ten yards.

12. Don't draw an offsides penalty. Stay behind the 40-yard line until the football has been kicked.

13. Huddle before each kickoff to determine in what general direction the ball will be kicked and what style of coverage will be used.

14. If the kickoff man seldom gets height or distance on his kickoffs, let him try laying the football flat on the ground sidewise. This type of kick is often difficult to catch and allows members of the kickoff team to penetrate deeper downfield before the football is caught.

15. If the game is being filmed, instruct the cameramen to get a wide-angle look at the kickoff team as they cover the kickoff. This can later be used as an instructional aid for teaching staying in lanes, etc.

16. If the kickoff receiving team generally uses only one style of return (such as up the middle), position the strongest kickoff team tacklers so they will be covering that area.

3

The Kickoff Return
Special Team

IMPORTANCE OF THE KICKOFF RETURN TEAM

The kickoff return is one of the most exciting plays in football. Because of the spread-out, wide-open style of action, the kickoff return team has good opportunity to accumulate a sizable amount of yardage. For every ten yards gained by the return team, the offensive team has one less first down to make. A poor return places the offensive team in a position where their choice of plays is limited. A good return gives the offensive team room to strike, using almost any offensive play they choose. Even if the offense is forced to punt, they will be in position to kick deep into their opponent's territory.

PERSONNEL NEEDED

The basic needs for any style of kickoff return are (1) five front line blockers, (2) two ends, and (3) four backs. Some coaches may prefer to have six backs in the return lineup, replacing the two ends with backs. Having six backs insures having a good ball carrier handle the kickoff. All backs, with the possible exception of the deepest backs, must be willing blockers. All backs must be able to catch the football and not likely to fumble when hit.

The front five are chosen for their open field blocking ability. The coach must never feel he has to have two tackles, two guards and one center in the five blocking positions. Select the best blockers regardless of offensive position. Even use backs on the front line if they are good open field blockers.

Get as much speed as possible into the return team. Blocks must be made quickly and the football advanced upfield as rapidly as possible to get maximum yardage. Members of the return team must be aggressive and must like to hit.

FACTORS AFFECTING THE POSITIONING OF KICKOFF RETURN TEAM PLAYERS

Regardless of the style of kickoff return a team uses, there are certain factors that determine the positioning of the return team players. These factors are as follows:

Wind. When the kickoff return team is facing the wind they should expect the kick to carry deeper than usual. Move all players, except the front five, back several steps. When the wind is to their backs, kickoff return team members should expect the football not to carry as far. Move up and be ready for a shorter kick.

Rain. Heavy rain could cause a football to be kicked shorter than usual. Even if it isn't raining at the moment of the kickoff the football might be wet and heavy from earlier in the game. Expecting a shorter kick, players should move up.

Ability of Kicker. Use scouting reports to determine the general distance and range of the opponent's kickoff man. Also watch him carefully in pre-game practice. Return players other than the front five move according to kicker's ability.

Score of the Game. During a close ball game, especially in the third or fourth quarter, the return team should watch for the onside kick. When anticipating an onside kick move all players much closer to the football than normal. If the opposition has the lead, especially late in the game, look for a long kick.

SETTING UP THE KICKOFF RETURN

There are any number of kickoff return styles, all of which have merit. We feel that every team should be prepared to run several styles of returns. If the same return style is used every week it will be relatively easy for the opposition to stop it.

Figure 3-1 illustrates a kickoff return *up the middle*. We feel that this is the safest of all returns. There is no wasted time involved. With reasonable blocking it will consistently get good return yardage. In fact, we have broken more returns up the middle for touchdowns than from any other style of kickoff return. When using the up-the-middle return, position the front five blockers above the 45-yard line. The two ends should be near the 30-yard line and at least 6 to 7 yards in from the sideline. (**Note:** Never let the ends make the mistake of lining up 2 or 3 yards from the sideline. They can cover much more territory by moving away from the sideline.) Two backs should be near the 25-yard line and near the center of the field. The two deep backs are stationed between the 5- and 10-yard lines. (All players other than the front five may need to move up or back depending on the kicking ability of the opposing kicker.)

Blocking assignments for the up-the-middle return are as follows:

Front five:

Center. Drop back with the kick, then block the kicker. Take him either way he can be taken (left or right). Stay with him until the play ends.

Left guard. Drop back according to depth of the kick; cut across the field and block the *second* man on the far side of the football.

Left tackle. Drop back according to depth of the kick; cut across the field and block the *first* man on the far side of the football.

Right guard. Drop back according to depth of the kick; cut across the field and block the *second* man on the far side of the football.

Right tackle. Drop back according to the depth of the kick; cut across the field and block the *first* man on the far side of the football.

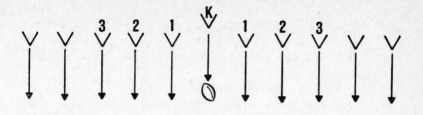

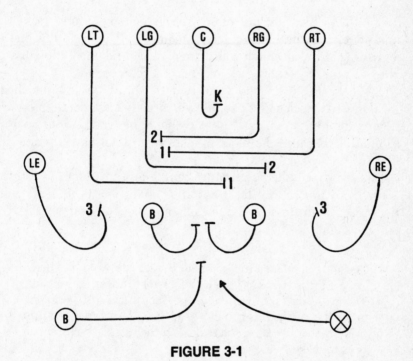

FIGURE 3-1

Ends:

Left end. Start to the inside of the field, then turn back towards the sideline and block the *third* man on your side of the football.

Right end. Start to the inside of the field, then turn back towards the sideline and block the *third* man on your side of the football.

Backs:

> *Two middle backs.* Drop back slightly with the kick, then
> lead ball carrier up the middle, blocking any opposing
> players who enter the lane and are in position to make
> the tackle.
>
> *Two deep backs.* One back calls for the ball and catches it.
> The other back checks for a fumble, then leads up the
> middle, blocking the first player who threatens the ball
> carrier.

If the kick goes to one of the front five men, he must make the
quick decision whether to catch it or simply fall on it. Falling on the
football is safer, although some linemen will be good enough athletes to catch the short kick and make a few yards.

When the kick goes to an end, he must go straight ahead
gaining what yardage he can (he will already have good field position by catching the kick). The end should never attempt to cut up
the middle because the blocking pattern will not have formed this
soon.

The two middle backs must handle all short kicks in front of
them. They must never let the football bounce past them, allowing
the kickoff team to advance farther into their territory before the
ball is caught.

> *Coaching point:* Instruct the middle backs never to backpedal
> in an effort to catch on the fly a kick that is over their heads.
> This will cause confusion with the deep backs as to who will
> make the catch. *Always* allow the deep backs to run up to
> make the catch rather than allowing the middle backs to run
> back to make it.

The deep backs must attempt to catch the football before it
hits the ground. If the ball hits the ground it can take some strange
bounces. Once the ball is caught the runner sprints straight up the
middle. Heading for the sidelines is dangerous for there is no
blocking there.

Figure 3-2 shows another type of return up the middle of the
field. *Wedge* blocking is used here. The *wedge* return utilizes five
front line blockers, four secondary blockers and two deep backs
This return works best when facing a kicker who consistently kicks

Wedge return

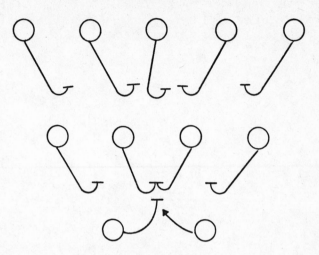

FIGURE 3-2

deep to one of the backs rather than short to one of the nine blockers. Blocking assignments for the wedge return are relatively simple. No blocker is assigned a particular man to block. As the ball is kicked, the front five blockers drop back 5 to 10 yards, closing in towards each other until they are 3 to 5 yards apart. They then begin moving forward as a unit, blocking the first defenders coming up the middle. The four secondary blockers drop back with the kick, closing in to within 2 or 3 yards of each other. They are to drop back until they are between 5 and 10 yards in front of the back who receives the football. As the catch is made they lead the ball carrier up the middle, blocking (to the outside if possible) the first defensive men in the area.

> *Coaching point*: These four blockers will probably not be as fast as the ball carrier, so they must be careful not to set up too close to the back catching the ball. If this is done, the back might have to slow down to keep from running over his block-ers.

The deep back who does not handle the kick must wait along-side the receiver to check for a fumble. Once the ball has been safely caught, this back serves as a personal escort for the ball carrier. He must block the first defender who threatens the ball carrier.

Stress with all blockers that they must *never* pass up the opportunity to block the *first man* who threatens the ball carrier (see Figure 3-3).

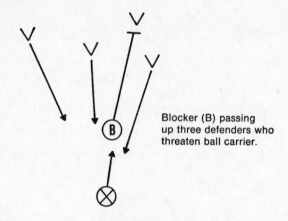

Blocker (B) passing up three defenders who threaten ball carrier.

FIGURE 3-3

If the football is kicked to one of the secondary blockers, the player catching the ball has two options: (1) run with it up the middle, gaining as much yardage as possible, or (2) toss the ball to one of the deep backs. Both options must be practiced.

Figure 3-4 shows a *sideline* return. There are several blocking patterns that can be used on this return. Each coach should make minor adjustments to suit his taste. The sideline return may be used with a deep back reverse or with no reverse pattern.

The return shown here is to the receiving team's right. As the ball is kicked the *right tackle* turns to his right and sprints down the sideline, judging the depth of the kick. He must be very careful not to outrun the kick, and should stop short of the depth of the receiver. He then positions himself no closer than 5 yards and no farther than 8 yards from the sideline. The *right guard, center, left guard,* and *left tackle* turn to their right and follow the right tackle down the sideline, with each man setting up no closer than 5 yards to the player in front (see Figure 3-4 for correct alignment). The job of these five men is to remain in their positions until the ball carrier starts down the sideline, behind their wall. As the defenders close

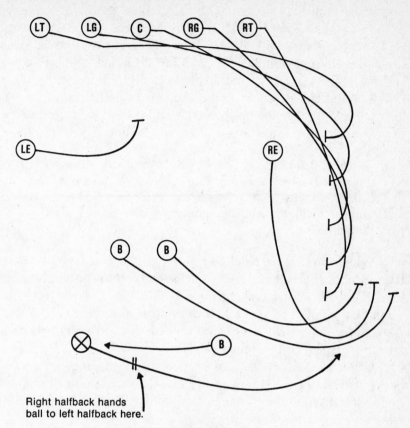

Right halfback hands
ball to left halfback here.

FIGURE 3-4

in to make the tackle these five blockers must block the nearest defender in their area. Do not let any defender penetrate this solid five-man wall without blocking him.

The job of the *right end*, after checking for a short kick, is to drop back and become the first blocker behind the wall. The two *middle backs* should drop back with the kick and also lead the ball carrier behind the wall. **Note:** If the right end or the middle backs see a defender closing in on the ball carrier they must block him whether they have reached the wall or not.

The *left end* does not attempt to get behind the return wall. His duty is to sprint to the middle of the field, locating the fastest defender downfield and blocking him. This will give the other return team members more time to set up the wall.

When running a reverse with the sideline return (as in Figure 3-4) stress these points:

1. On a return right, the left back will carry the football. If the ball is kicked to the left back, he is to sprint towards the wall, going *in front* of the right back and faking the ball to him.

2. If the ball is kicked to the right back, he is to sprint to his left, going in front of the left back. He hands the football to the left back and carries out his fake up the left sideline.

> *Coaching point*: The left back must be coached not to reach the right back immediately after the right back catches the ball. There must be time for the right back to begin his sprint to the left with the football, in order to draw the defenders in that direction.

When running the sideline return *without a reverse*, one deep back catches the ball and the other leads him up the sideline behind the wall, after checking for a fumble. Deep backs must be reminded to call for the football to avoid mishandling the kickoff.

(**Note**: The sideline return *to the left* can be run by reversing assignments shown in Figure 3-4.)

Other kickoff returns can be designed, utilizing three deep backs instead of two. However, we feel that two good runners can do the job, freeing the third player for a blocking assignment elsewhere.

METHOD OF TEACHING THE KICKOFF RETURN

We have found the following method beneficial in teaching the kickoff return:

1. Diagram the entire return on the blackboard so that the team can see it. The coach may choose to mimeograph the return and hand out copies. Either way helps players understand the overall design of the return.

2. Position the players on the field, showing them exactly where to line up and why. Show them how to make allowances for the wind, etc.

3. Walk each player through his assignments.

4. Send a dummy kickoff team walking down the field. Let the return team walk through their assignments.

5. Let the kickoff team and the return team jog one-half speed through the return. Kickoff team members are to stop when confronted by a blocker.

6. Practice the return full speed. This is necessary in order to develop a good return team. However, spring practice and early fall practice are the best times to perfect the return. Due to the injury risk factor some coaches are reluctant to practice the return full speed once the season has started.

COACHING POINTS FOR THE KICKOFF RETURN TEAM

1. Once the blockers have seen that the kickoff has been caught, they should never look back at the ball carrier. They must block until they hear the whistle, trusting the ball carrier to follow their blocks.

2. Never let the football hit the ground on the kickoff. Catch the ball on the fly. Once it touches the ground it may be difficult to pick up.

3. Work with all receivers to make sure they cradle the football securely to prevent a fumble.

4. Make sure all players understand the clipping penalty. Work hard to avoid this very costly mistake.

5. Teach the players to use good judgment as to when to field the football kicked near the sideline, and when to let it go out of bounds. Make sure the players understand that a kickoff is a *live* ball and can be recovered by the kickoff team after it goes 10 yards.

6. Deep backs should be drilled on when to allow a deep kickoff to go into the end zone and when to field it.

7. Kickoff return players must not line up too near the sidelines before the football is kicked. There is little action here as compared to the middle areas of the field.

8. If the kickoff team draws a penalty (offsides) on the kickoff, accept the penalty if (a) the kick was deep and the runback was short, (b) the kickoff went into the end zone, or (c) the kickoff was fumbled and lost. Decline the penalty if (a) the kick was returned for good yardage, or (b) weather conditions are poor and the chance of a fumble on another return is likely.

9. The return team should huddle before each kickoff to make sure all members know which return will be used. Also, use this time to talk over any unusual situation that might affect the kick,

such as wind, rain, injury to regular kickers, possibility of onside kick, etc.

10. Don't be afraid to teach several types of returns. Although all of them won't be used in every game, the variety will be useful throughout the long season.

11. Sometimes a return will be planned but the ball kicked short or to someone other than the deep or middle backs. When this occurs the one catching the football must get maximum yardage straight up the field as quickly as possible. He must not delay, waiting for a return pattern to form.

12. When a sideline return is planned (and there is to be no reverse or fake reverse), the runner should fake a run up the middle before cutting behind his wall of blockers (see Figure 3-5). This will draw the defenders towards the *inside* of the field. As the ball carrier cuts behind the return wall, the tacklers will turn towards the sideline and, hopefully, into a solid wall of blockers.

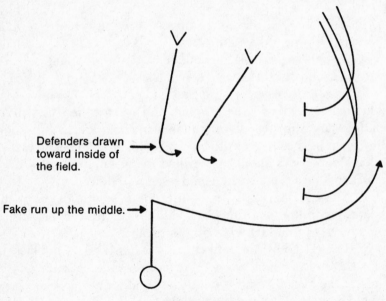

Defenders drawn toward inside of the field.

Fake run up the middle.

FIGURE 3-5

13. When there is to be a reverse or fake reverse on the return, the man catching the kickoff always goes in front (nearest the tacklers) of the back who is to be given the ball or faked to (see Figure 3-6)

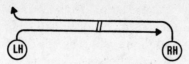

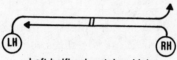

Right halfback catches kick;
hands off or fakes to left half.

Left halfback catches kick;
hands off or fakes to right half.

FIGURE 3-6

14. If the ball is kicked between the middle and deep backs, always let the deep backs come up and make the catch, rather than allowing the middle backs to backpedal to make the catch. This is awkward for the middle backs and might result in a fumble. Also, if a middle back handles the kick, the deep backs will be *behind* him and will be unable to block in front of him. (See Figure 3-7.)

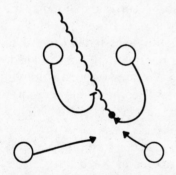
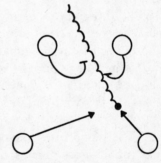

WRONG — middle back making the catch in front of the deep back.

CORRECT — middle back allowing deep back to come up and make the catch.

FIGURE 3-7

15. The return team should be prepared to set up sideline returns to the *left* as well as to the right.

16. Give blockers plenty of practice in executing their open field, kickoff return blocks. This can be done using large stand-up

dummies or by using players holding small hand dummies as blocking targets. This eliminates much of the risk of injury.

17. The coach should review the kickoff return patterns in detail several times during the season. A player who is coached early in the season to set up a wall 7 yards from the sideline may, by mid-season, be setting it up 12 yards from the sideline.

18. Even the hardest working kickoff return teams may go several games or perhaps a whole season without returning a kickoff for a touchdown. To keep the players from becoming discouraged the coach should point out specific cases where good returns have placed the ball in excellent field position which led later to a touchdown.

19. The coach should instruct the cameramen filming the games to take wide-angle pictures of the kickoff return so that blocking assignments and techniques can be studied by the coach and players.

20. If the ball carrier breaks into the clear and is obviously headed for a touchdown, all blocking attempts must stop. There are few things in football more discouraging than having a touchdown called back because of an unnecessary block behind the ball carrier.

21. Although a special onside kick receiving team may be available, the regular receiving team should be drilled on handling an onside kick. One front line player should be assigned the task of alerting his front line teammates to be ready for the onside kick.

22. When blockers are setting up a wall along the sideline, they must be patient and allow tacklers to "come to them" rather than leaving the wall and "going after the tacklers." (See Figure 3-8.)

23. The biggest mistake of many blockers is running past several potential tacklers near the ball carrier and blocking a less dangerous defender farther downfield.

24. Have substitutes well prepared so there will be no breakdown in the return pattern when a replacement is in the game.

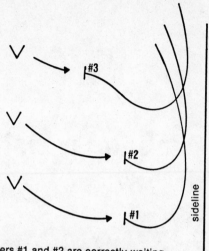

Blockers #1 and #2 are correctly waiting at the wall for defenders to come to them. Blocker #3 is INCORRECTLY going after the defender, creating a break in the wall.

FIGURE 3-8

4

The Punting Special Team

SELECTING A SNAPPER

It is a mistake to think that the regular offensive center *has* to be the snapper for punts. Making a short snap to a quarterback in the T-formation style ball exchange takes a completely different skill from that needed to center a football 10-14 yards back to a punter. While it is true that the regular offensive center must have a number of the basic skills required of a snapper, he still must not be pushed into the job. It is a good idea to test every player on the team for this special job—backs, ends, receivers, defensive linemen, etc. The best snapper I ever had was a tight end.

Other than being able to physically snap the ball in the manner desired by the coach, the snapper should have the following qualities:

1. He must be able to block.
2. He must be able to think.
3. He must not be one who panics in a close game.
4. He must be willing to work to perfect his skill.
5. He should be able to cover punts and tackle, although this should not be considered as important as making an accurate snap.

SELECTING A PUNTER

During the first day or two of punter tryouts, the coach will probably notice several kids with strong legs who occasionally get good distance on their kicks. As will be mentioned later, a strong kicking leg is a main requirement for a good punter. But there are many more requisites to being a punter than many of these potential punters will have.

A good punter will develop a punting *style*. This style should not vary from kick to kick. We teach our punters to position themselves with the left foot slightly forward (for a right-footed kicker). After receiving the snap from center the punter steps with his right foot, then his left, before punting the football. When developing his punting style, the punter must be aware of the distance of the drop of the football from his hands to his foot. This drop must remain the same for each kick. Young punters especially may not be aware of the importance of dropping the ball properly.

A good punter must be able to maintain *distance consistency*. A punter who booms one kick 40 yards and the next one 17 yards is more a hindrance than a help to the kicking game.

Height consistency is also important. The higher the kick, the more time the punting team will have to get downfield before the catch is made. The coach must select the punter with the best combination of height *and* distance.

Accuracy of punts is next in importance in selecting a punter. Although, in reality, making an accurate punt to a designated spot is extremely difficult when facing a hard rushing defense, some punters will be able to do this better than others. So before making the final selection of a punter, let all candidates kick under pressure.

Maneuverability is important, for the punter may be called on to catch high or low snaps as well as snaps far to the right or left. When two punters of equal kicking ability are available, choose the one with the best reactions.

The physical size of the punter is not important although a strong leg is of course necessary. A tall punter gives the snapper a better target, but this should be considered an added luxury rather than the deciding factor in choosing a punter. Be sure the punter likes to kick and will work at it. This is a skill that can be practiced at any time, alone if necessary. All that is needed is a punter, a football, and a desire to improve.

OTHER PUNTING TEAM PERSONNEL

The *offensive line* of the punting team may consist of regular offensive linemen or of players especially chosen for the punting team. We have often used backs on the offensive line to get more speed on the punting team. The offensive linemen should be selected for their ability to do these things:

1. Make solid blocking contact.
2. Hold this contact for the length of time it takes to count "1001. . .1002."
3. Release and sprint downfield full speed.
4. Locate the football and come under control near the ball carrier.
5. Make the tackle.

The *blocking back* positions can be filled with backs or with ends, tackles, or guards. They must be able to perform the same five previously mentioned skills as the offensive linemen. They must use good judgment in selecting whom to block. Any defensive men coming up the middle should be blocked first as they pose the biggest threat to blocking a punt.

PUNTING FOR ACCURACY

Although the punter should have a general idea where he desires each kick to land, there are two occasions when an especially accurate punt is needed:

1. when the football is kicked out-of-bounds, and
2. when the football is kicked dead inside the 10-yard line.

When *kicking out-of-bounds* follow these steps:

1. Take the snap from center in the normal fashion.
2. The first step should angle the body in the exact direction on the yard line where the kicker wants the ball to go out-of-bounds.
3. Kick the football straight as with a normal kick, except this time the angle of the body will direct the football out-of-bounds.
4. Use reason when picking the spot where the ball is to go

out-of-bounds. If the kicker is on the 50-yard line and his normal range is 35 yards, he should aim for the 15-yard line and not the 3-yard line.

5. Remember to kick the ball with power. It will be marked where the ball leaves the field, not how far it travels.
6. Allow for a reasonable margin of error. If the punter is kicking to his *left* sideline, and aims for the 1-yard line, any slight punting error to the right will take the football into the end zone.
7. Height is not important when kicking out-of-bounds. However the punter must be careful not to alter his style to avoid a high kick.

When attempting to kick the ball *dead inside the 10-yard line*, keep these points in mind:

1. Make sure an attempted kick inside the opponent's 10-yard line is within range of the punter. Generally speaking, the football should be on the opponent's side of the 50-yard line before a kick of this type is attempted.
2. The closer the kick is made to the opponent's goal line, the less the chance it will be handled. This, of course, is due to the fear of fumbling the ball.
3. The punt should be high, assuring the punting team time to be downfield when the ball hits the ground.
4. The ball should be kicked "soft" to lessen its chances of going into the end zone on the fly or the bounce.
5. As the football hits the ground the members of the punting team should surround it, allowing it to roll as close to the goal line as possible before downing it. Communication between players may help prevent one player from downing the ball prematurely. (*Examples:* "Let it roll," or "It's on the 5. . . the 4. . . the 3. . . the 2. . .down it!")
6. If the football hits a member of the receiving team intentionally or unintentionally, recover it immediately.
7. Surrounding the football as it rolls goalward helps prevent a receiver from suddenly scooping up the ball and making an attempted runback.

Remember that kicking out-of-bounds and kicking inside the 10-yard line both require constant practice by the punter and punting team members.

SNAPPING AND PUNTING A WET FOOTBALL

Rain on a game night after weeks of clear weather practice can be very dangerous unless the snapper and punter are accustomed to handling a wet football. There are two ways to be prepared for this situation. First, make sure that on rainy practice days the punting game is built into the practice schedule. (**Note:** If no punting practice was planned for the rainy day's workout, it could be quickly substituted into the schedule in place of some other drill that can be done in wet or dry weather.) Punting and snapping in the rain at practice is the best way to create confidence in these players and calm their fear of handling the wet football. The second preparation for handling the wet ball is to soak an old football in a bucket of water on days when the weather is clear. At the end of each punting practice insert the wet football, allowing all snappers and punters to handle it several times. The coach may want the punter to move up a yard or two nearer the snapper to ease the pressure of making a long snap. The punter should also be reminded to kick from an area that provides the best footing for his kicking steps, especially if the ground is slippery.

PUNTING UNDER PRESSURE

We feel that no coach should make his final selection of his punter until he sees them under pressure of a heavy defensive rush. Work up to a heavy punt rush by using these four steps: (1) Let the punter take the snap and send two or three defenders half speed across the line as he kicks. This trains the punter to keep his eyes on the football and not the defenders. (2) Using the drill shown in Figure 4-1, send three defenders rushing the kicker. Three blockers provide protection. (3) Send five defenders against five blockers from the right side of the punter (see Figure 4-2). Repeat from the left side of the punter. (4) Now send from seven to ten defenders against a full punting team of blockers. Defenders should alternate methods of attempting to block the kick.

If a punter continues to perform poorly under pressure, he must be replaced. A less talented punter who can stand up under pressure will, in the long run, prove more valuable to the team.

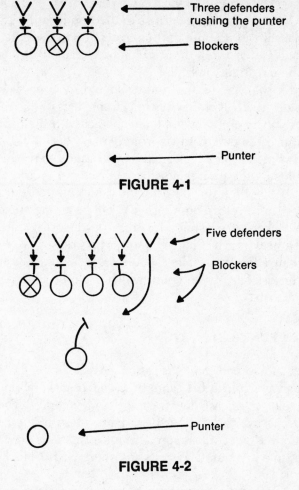

FIGURE 4-1

FIGURE 4-2

PREPARING FOR A BAD SNAP

The punter should not *expect* a bad snap from center, but should *be prepared* if the snap is not right on target. We drill for the bad snap by having a center purposely make bad snaps to the punter in practice. The bad snaps should be to the punter's left, to his right, low or into the ground, and above his head.

The biggest mistake made in handling a bad snap to the right or left is not getting the body in front of the ball. Since the snap must travel 10 to 14 yards (according to the depth of the punter), there is ample time for the punter to move a step to the right or left so that the ball will arrive in front of his body. This will block the ball in case he does not catch it.

When the snap is low the punter should drop his body and attempt to block the ball with his hands, arms, legs or chest. However, he must be careful to avoid knee contact with the ground as this would cause the official to rule the play dead.

The only defense for a high snap is good hands. If the ball goes through the hands the punter must retrieve it and then make the decision as to whether to still attempt a kick or to run. If the receiving team has a return on, there may not be enough defenders rushing the kicker to prevent him from getting the kick away. However, if a heavy rush is on, the punter may do well to retrieve the ball, pick up a few yards if he can, and be tackled. At least there will not be the risk of a blocked punt which could be picked up and turned into a score.

THE SPREAD PUNT FORMATION

We feel the spread punt formation provides enough time to get the kick away while at the same time enabling the members of the punting team to release downfield for punt coverage. There are any number of ways to position the players when using a spread punt formation. However, all spread punt formations are alike in that the offensive linemen take splits anywhere from 18 inches to 3 feet or more.

Figure 4-3 shows a spread punt formation using seven linemen, three backs and a punter. The blocking backs should be five yards deep. If the punter is right-footed the two blocking backs should be on the right side with the single blocking back on the left side. (Reverse for a left-footed kicker.) Blocking rules for the linemen in any spread punt formation are as follows:

1. Block the defender head-on. If no defender is head-on, block the first man to the outside.
2. If two defenders line up in the gap to the inside, call "Help." This means for the man calling "help" and all those outside him to block inside (see Figure 4-4).

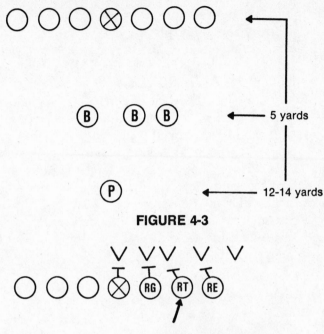

SPREAD PUNT

FIGURE 4-3

Right tackle sees two
defenders to his inside;
calls "HELP!" RT and RE now
block inside.

FIGURE 4-4

The job of the blocking backs is to block the first man to threaten the punter. When the ball is snapped they should all look first in the area over center and guard. If no one is coming through here check over the tackle, then the end, and finally to the outside. Instruct the blocking backs never to back up. This would place them too near the punter and might result in their being hit by the ball after it is punted.

As soon as the football has been punted, the front seven linemen must fan out and cover in lanes with no one player trailing another. The ends must be responsible for outside containment. The left blocking back trails the left tackle downfield while the right blocking back follows the right tackle. The middle blocking back follows the center straight downfield (the center has no block-ing responsibility unless a man is directly over him). The punter then takes the job of a "safety man" and is the last man downfield, being careful to stay between the ball carrier and the goal line.

The coach may choose to split the end on the side of the two blocking backs. This might allow him to release faster downfield to cover the punt. The two blocking backs should be able to take care of the defenders rushing from that side.

Figure 4-5 shows another style of spread punt formation. The guards split an extra 2 feet from the center. Two blocking backs cover these areas and line up about 2 yards deep. These two backs and all linemen use the blocking rules described earlier (head-on. . . outside. . . "help" if two defenders are in the inside gap). The third blocking back lines up 5-6 yards deep and offers personal protection for the punter who is 12-14 yards deep. After the kick the linemen cover by fanning to the outside. The two close blocking backs follow the tackles, and the single blocking back trails the center.

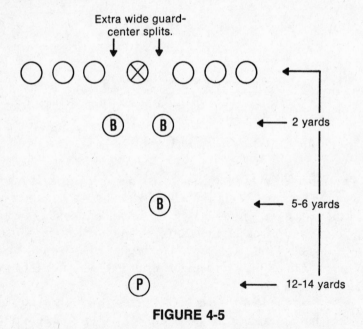

FIGURE 4-5

Figure 4-6 illustrates a spread punt formation with two split ends. Their purpose is to sprint immediately to the punt receiver and make the tackle. They must be fast and sure tacklers. The guards, tackles, and center follow regular blocking rules. The two backs just outside the tackles follow the same blocking rules as the linemen (head-on. . . outside. . . "help"). The personal blocker for the punter is 5-6 yards deep.

Remember: The spread punt formation offers the best way to combine *good blocking protection* with *good punt coverage capable of stopping the runback.*

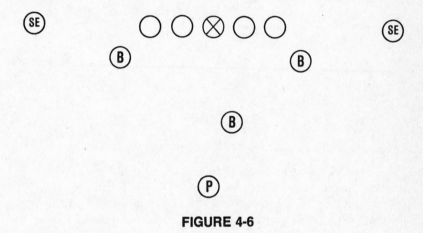

FIGURE 4-6

THE TIGHT PUNT FORMATION

The tight punt formation should be used when expecting an all-out rush by the defensive team in an attempt to block the punt. It provides maximum protection for the punter, but does not allow the punting team to cover the kick as thoroughly as from the spread formation. The tight punt formation is often used when punting from inside the 15-yard line. It is in this type of situation that the defensive team is most likely to attempt to block the punt. Figure 4-7 shows the tight punt formation. The blocking rule for the linemen is to block the first man inside. If no defender is inside, block head-on. The center blocks head-on or releases. The two wingbacks follow the same "inside. . . head-on" rule as the linemen. The personal blocker in front of the punter blocks the first man to threaten the kicker. The punter must not line up as deep as on the spread formation. Between 9 and 11 yards will place the punter in the middle of the "pocket protection" as he kicks.

TIGHT PUNT

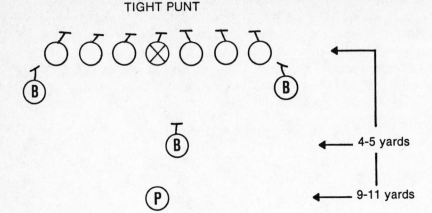

FIGURE 4-7

Coaching point: If the punter is kicking out of his end zone and the snap is bad, he may be wise to fall on the ball for a two-point safety rather than risk getting the punt blocked, resulting in a touchdown (six points). The score and time left in the game will be the deciding factor in this decision. Have the punter practice falling on the ball in the end zone in daily drills so there will be no doubt as to what he must do if the coach calls for this play in a game.

Once the ball has been safety kicked from the tight punt formation, the two wingbacks and seven linemen must fan out and cover as much of the field as possible as they sprint after the punt receiver. The blocking back and punter serve as "safety men," staying between the ball carrier and the goal line.

TELLING TEAMMATES WHERE BALL WILL BE KICKED

In the huddle, prior to the kick, the punter should give the punting team members information about where the ball will be kicked. He might tell them the ball will be kicked to the *right* or *left*, to the *wide* or *short* side of the field, *high* (near the opponent's goal) or *long* when kicking from his own end of the field). If the wind will be a factor in the kick or if rain will limit the distance of the kick, this information should be passed along to the punting team members. The punter may be trying to punt away from the opponent's best punt return man. Whatever the reason, it will help those covering to have an idea where the football will land.

COVERING THE PUNT

All players on the punting team should observe these rules when covering a punt:

1. Whatever the punting formation, the players should fan out, covering as much territory as possible as they sprint downfield.
2. After leaving the line of scrimmage look up and find the ball. Judge its height, distance and direction, and sprint to the area where it should land. Do not keep looking up for the ball after the first time. This slows the runner down.
3. Don't overrun the ball and end up behind the ball carrier.
4. Come under control when nearing the ball carrier.
5. Surround the receiver on all front sides, not giving him running room in any direction.
6. If the ball hits the ground without being caught, surround it and let it roll as long as it is rolling towards the opponent's goal.
7. Watch for a fair catch by the receiver.
8. If the ball hits the ground, do not relax until the whistle blows, although it may not appear that anyone will pick up the ball and run with it.
9. Watch for a reverse or trick play.
10. Make sure one player (usually the punter) has been designated to cover the punt slowly, making the tackle and preventing the touchdown only if all others have failed to stop the ball carrier.

PUNTING ON THIRD DOWN

There are situations where punting on third down is advantageous:

1. Third and long yardage inside the offensive team's 15-yard line. (A bad snap or fumble would not be fatal, as fourth down could still be used as punting down.)

2. If the game is close and the defense is playing well, but the offense can't move the ball, punt on third down and hope the receiving team makes a mistake.
3. If rain is a factor, the ball may be hard to snap and handle. Fourth down still remains in case the third down snap is mishandled.
4. At the end of the first and third quarters, punt on third down to take advantage of a strong wind before the quarter changes.

Never punt on third down (1) when trailing in score with only a few minutes to play, (2) when leading by a large margin and a fumble or mishandled snap will not be too costly, or (3) if the offensive team has been moving the ball well.

CONDITIONING THE PUNTING TEAM

Members of the punting team must be sold on the idea that the faster they get the ball carrier the less return yardage he will have. It is the tendency of some players who are not well coached or in condition to ease up as they go downfield to cover the punt. In practicing the punt coverage and in running sprints, make sure the players go full speed. The amount of conditioning necessary for punting team members will depend on how many of them are regulars on the offensive or defensive teams. If the punting team is made up of players who are not regulars, they should be fresh and well rested. However, if the punting team members are regulars they will need more conditioning than other players. Running sprints just for the sake of running sprints is fine. However, these players will have a better attitude if the sprints become a learning situation with the punters kicking, the centers snapping, and the coaches working on punt coverage fundamentals as these players get in their extra work.

5

The Punt Return
Special Team

SELECTING PUNT RETURN TEAM MEMBERS

Members of the punt return team belong to either of two groups: (1) those who handle the punt, and (2) those who block.

The main requirements for those handling the punts are the ability to consistently catch any type of punt (spiral, end-over-end, low, high, etc), and to get good return yardage after catching the ball. There will be from one to five of these players in the lineup, depending on the style of return. These players need not all be backs. Wide receivers and tight ends can be used here. They should also be willing to block when not carrying the football. Make sure these punt handlers are well tested under fire in practice. Handling a punt with 11 defenders bearing down full speed upon the receiver is one of the most difficult assignments in football. If necessary, sacrifice running ability in order to have the kick handled by a receiver who is not likely to panic.

When selecting blockers for the punt return team, make sure to select players who are able and willing to make open field blocks rather than on-the-line-of-scrimmage blocks. These players must be willing to work hard learning to set up the returns correctly. Quickness, more than size, is important, for the players will not only set up return walls, but will often lead the defense in rushing the punter. Although size isn't too important, make sure the team isn't so small that opponents frequently fake a punt and run a power play at the undersized defense.

SETTING UP THE PUNT RETURN WALL

Most punt return teams consist of three areas. First, there are the front line players on the line of scrimmage. There will be from four to eight of these players. Their main job will be to set up a sideline wall, to hold the punting team's linemen up at the line of scrimmage delaying them from getting downfield fast, or on occasion, to rush the punter. The second line of players, ranging in number from one to four, are positioned off the line of scrimmage up to a depth of 20 to 25 yards. The job of these players is to handle (or fair catch) all short punts, to watch for a fake punt and pass, to keep teammates away from a short kick that has hit the ground and is bouncing around, and to block if the punt is long and is being handled by a deep back. Finally, there are the deep receiving backs. There will be from one to three of these depending on the style of return and the preference of the coach. Their job is to handle the punt on the fly before it has a chance to hit the ground and bounce around towards their own goal. Deep backs must have good hands and use good judgment in catching the punts.

Figure 5-1 shows how to set up a punt return wall with a reverse (or fake reverse) by the deep backs. Individual assignments are as follows for a return to the right (reverse all procedures for a return left):

Right end: Line up on outside shoulder of offensive end. Hand shiver the offensive end and lead down the sideline. Watch the depth of the kick and set up the wall about 5-8 yards from the sideline. Be careful not to set up the wall deeper than the ball has been kicked.

Right tackle: Line up head-on the offensive tackle. Hand shiver the tackle and follow the right end down the sideline. Set up the wall about 5-6 yards from the right end.

Right guard: Line up head-on the offensive guard. Hand shiver the guard and follow the tackle down the sideline. Set up about 5-6 yards from the tackle.

Left guard: Line up head-on the offensive guard. Hand shiver

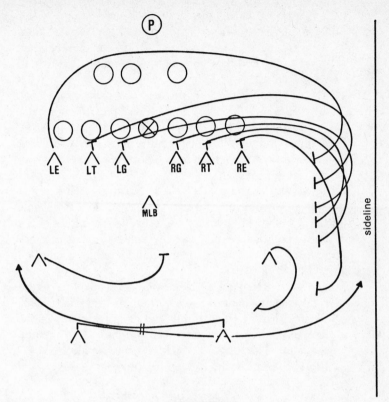

FIGURE 5-1

the guard and follow the right guard down the sideline,
setting up about 5-6 yards behind him.

*Left tackle:*Line up head-on the offensive tackle. Hand shiver
the tackle and follow the left guard down the sideline,
setting up about 5-6 yards from him.

*Left end:*Line up on the outside shoulder of the offensive end.
Hand shiver the end and rush the punter. Attempt to
pressure him into making a bad punt. After the ball is
kicked, head down the sideline and set up as the final
man in the six-man wall. **Note**: Place a very responsible
player at this position. He must never let the punter fake
a kick and run around him for first-down yardage. He
must rush the punter from the outside!

Middle linebacker: Watch for a fake punt and run up the middle. If this does not occur, block the snapper and detain
him from getting downfield.

Left middle-depth back: Line up 20 to 25 yards deep. Check
for a fake punt followed by a pass or run to your side.
After the ball has been kicked, drop back slightly, then
move to the middle of the field, blocking the first man to
show.

Right middle-depth back: Line up 20 to 25 yards deep. Check
for a fake punt followed by a run or pass to your side.
After the ball has been kicked, drop back towards the
first man in the wall. Block the first man to show. A block
in this area is often necessary before the ball carrier can
get behind the wall.

Right deep back: If the ball is kicked your way catch it, then,
moving to your left, hand the ball to the left deep back.
Carry out a fake to the left. Be sure to go in front of the
left deep back as you hand the ball to him. If the kick
goes to the left deep back, go behind him, fake a hand-off
and carry out a fake to the left.

Left deep back: If the ball is kicked your way, catch it and head
right towards the wall. Go in front of the right deep back,
faking the ball to him. If the right deep back handles the
kick, go behind him, take the hand-off and get behind
the wall. (The left deep back is receiving the ball on a
hand-off from the right deep back in Figure 5-1.)

Figure 5-2 shows a return with a double wall, one to the right
and one to the left. This allows the punt receiver to get behind a
wall quickly whether the ball is kicked to the right or the left side of
the field. The punting team must guard against a return to either
side. Assignments for the double-return wall are as follows:

Right end: Line up head-on the offensive end. Hand shiver the
end and lead down the right sideline. Watch the
depth of the punt and be careful not to set up the wall
closer than 5 yards or greater than 8 or 9 yards from
the sideline.

Right tackle: Line up head-on the offensive guard. Hand
shiver the guard and follow the right end. Set up the
wall about 5-7 yards from the right end.

Left tackle: Line up head-on the offensive guard. Hand shiver
the guard and follow the right tackle down the
sideline setting up about 5-7 yards from him.

Left end: Rush the punter from the outside. Make sure he gets

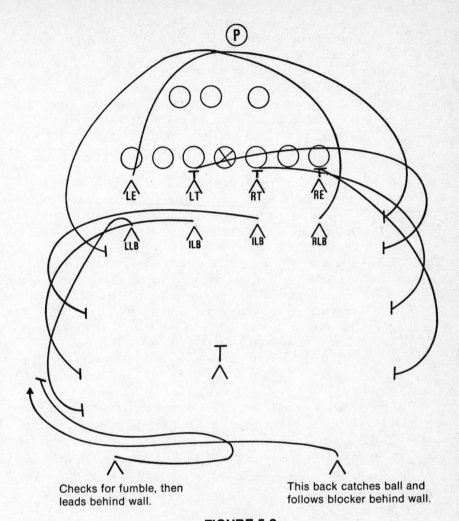

Checks for fumble, then
leads behind wall.

This back catches ball and
follows blocker behind wall.

FIGURE 5-2

the punt away and does not try to fake the punt and
run around end. After the kick, follow the left tackle
and set up the wall, being the last man in the wall on
the right side.

Left outside linebacker: Make a quick visual check to be sure
the punter has not received a bad snap. Sprint down
the left sideline, noting the depth of the punt. Set up
the wall on the left side between 5-8 yards from the
sideline.

Left inside linebacker: Follow the outside linebacker down the
left sideline, setting up the wall about 5-7 yards from
him.

Right inside linebacker: Follow the left inside linebacker down
the sideline, setting up about 5-7 yards from him.

Right outside linebacker: Rush the punter. Make sure he gets
the punt away and does not fake the punt and run
around end. After the kick, sprint down the left
sideline and become the last man in the wall to that
side.

Middle-depth back: Line up over the offensive center about
20-25 yards deep. Be ready to fair catch a short kick or
clear the area of teammates in case a short kick has hit
the ground and is bouncing around. If the kick is long,
block the first man downfield.

Two deep backs: After judging the direction of the punt, one
deep back is to call for the ball. The other deep back
checks for a fumble, then blocks the man nearest the
receiver. If no tackler is near the receiver, lead the
receiver (ball carrier) behind the wall on the side
nearest to where the ball was caught. (If desired, the
two deep backs could reverse or fake reverse before
getting behind a wall.)

If the coach does not wish to set up a wall he may still get a
good return by having his players hold the offensive linemen up on
the line of scrimmage as shown in Figure 5-3. The purpose of this is
to allow the punt receiver more time to make a safe catch without
having the punting team bear down on him. Set up the return in
the following manner:

1. Seven punt return team linemen line up head-on the seven
offensive linemen. On the snap of the ball, "block" the
offensive linemen with a high "pass protection" block. Try
to keep the offensive linemen from releasing off the line of
scrimmage. As the offensive linemen manage to release,
the blockers are to release with them and continue "blocking" them wherever they go on the field. The "blockers"
must avoid getting behind the offensive linemen where a
clip might be called.

2. One (or both) of the outside linebackers should rush the
punter while the other drops back and picks up any offen-

Short receiver

Deep receiver

FIGURE 5-3

sive lineman who has managed to free himself from a
"blocker."

3. The short receiving back should watch for a short kick and
   make a fair catch if possible. If the ball is kicked deep, he is
   to block the first opposing player to threaten the receiver.
4. The deep receiver must handle a long kick anywhere on the
   field. If the "blockers" have done their job he should have
   ample time to make the catch and look for daylight. The
   deep receiver should be a player who is one of the best, if
   not the best, open field runner on the team. Although the

receiver should have sufficient ability to handle punts, some teams will prefer this style of return because it allows the receiver more time to safely handle the punt.

UTILIZING THE FAIR CATCH

The hand signal for a fair catch has changed slightly over the years. Make sure the rule book is consulted for the proper signal and that it is taught correctly to any player who might be in position to make a fair catch.

A fair catch should be made when the kick is short and members of the punting team have covered well and are in the area as the ball descends. A fair catch will prevent the ball from hitting the ground and rolling towards the receiving team's goal, thereby losing valuable yardage for the receiving team.

A fair catch should be made when the ball is punted high, allowing the tacklers plenty of time to surround the receiver and prevent a possible runback.

A fair catch might also be considered when a heavy rush is being used against the punter. With a heavy rush it is not likely that there will be enough blockers to aid the receiver in making a return.

A fair catch should *seldom* be made inside the 10-yard line. Allow the ball to hit the ground and hopefully it will bounce into the end zone where it will be brought out to the 20-yard line. Never take a chance on a fumble in this area.

> *Coaching point:* If the weather is rainy and the ball is wet it would probably be better to leave the ball alone instead of trying to make the fair catch. There is no need to risk a fumble, since the ball probably would not bounce far on the wet turf anyway.

WAYS TO BLOCK A PUNT

There are occasions when the punt return specialty team will want to attempt to *block the punt* rather than set up a return. The attempted block must be done by design rather than allowing the players to rush in a disorganized manner if there is to be any chance of success.

Figure 5-4 illustrates a *five man overload to one side* rush.
(**Note:** The other six players will be placed according to the preference of the coach. Four or five can be along the line of scrimmage
and one or two deep to handle the punt if it is gotten away.) Player
#1 in the diagram is to rush from the outside, forcing the blocking
back on that side to block him to the outside. Player #5 is to line up
on the inside shoulder of the offensive end and fire the gap to the
inside, trying to make the end block him. Players #2, #3, and #4
are to rush as shown in the diagram, with #2 and #3 going *outside*
the offensive end and #4 heading *over* the offensive end. The
offensive end cannot possibly block more than one man, leaving
three others charging into the punting area.

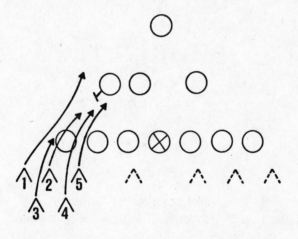

FIGURE 5-4

Figure 5-5 is a punt rush *up the middle* using four players (Position the other seven players according to preference of the coach.) Players #1 and #2 are to line up on the outside shoulders of the center. As he snaps the ball they are to drive into him, making sure he doesn't block anyone. Player #3 lines up head-on to outside shoulder of the left guard and fires the outside gap, forcing the guard to attempt to block him. Player #4 lines up behind players #1 and #2 and fires the gap to his right, heading straight up the middle.

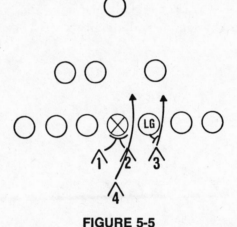

FIGURE 5-5

Figure 5-6 shows another *up the middle* rush, again using four defensive players. Players #1 and #2 line up on the outside shoulders of the offensive guards and fire outside, making the guards attempt to block them. Players #3 and #4 fire the center-guard gaps and head straight up the middle into the punting area.

Figure 5-7 illustrates an outside rush using only three men, rather than five as in the overload style rush. Player #1 rushes to the outside, forcing the blocking back to block him. Player #2 lines up head on to inside the offensive end and fires the inside gap, forcing the end to attempt to block him. Player #3 fires outside the end into the punting area.

All players chosen for the special punt-blocking team must possess strong determination and have a real desire to block the punt. The players must be warned against hitting the punter once the ball has been kicked. They must be taught to aim for a point where the ball meets the toe when attempting to block the punt.

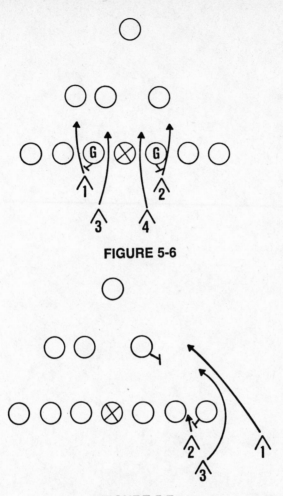

FIGURE 5-6

FIGURE 5-7

DANGERS TO AVOID WHEN ATTEMPTING TO BLOCK A PUNT

1. Players eager to block a punt will tend to *jump offsides* more than usual. They must be drilled to watch the football rather than listen for the snap count. Some teams will attempt to pull these eager players offside with a delayed snap count.
2. *Roughing the kicker* results in a penalty that usually gives the kicking team a first down. Remember—aim for the ball and not the body of the kicker.

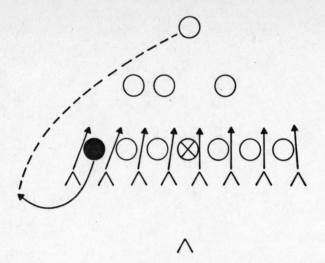

FIGURE 5-8

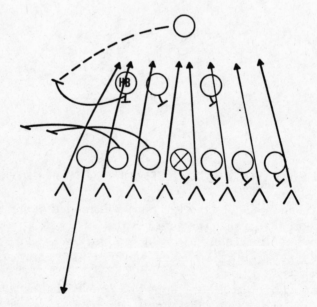

FIGURE 5-9

3. Watch for the *fake punt*. A pass to an end (Figure 5-8), a screen pass to a halfback (Figure 5-9), or a run (Figure 5-10) are all good plays against a team that rushes hard without watching for a fake punt.

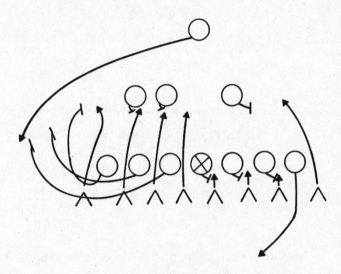

FIGURE 5-10

CONDITIONING THE PUNT RETURN TEAM

Setting up a return wall correctly takes plenty of full-speed running. Select players for the return team who can run without tiring too easily (**Example**: Heavier players, like tackles, will not always be able to go full speed.) If possible, select players for the return team who are not on the regular defensive team. This enables players to come off the bench fresh and well rested when the opponent punts. Practice setting up the wall each day. Insist that return team players (as well as others, of course) run wind sprints after practice full speed. Add additional sprints to return team members who do not tend to go all out when practicing the return. Getting in condition is mainly up to the player, once the coach has established his pattern of sprints. If any player fails to keep himself in top condition, the coach must look for a replacement.

6

The Extra Point
Special Team

FINDING A GOOD SNAPPER

There are three rules to follow when beginning the search for an extra point team center: (1) Don't assume the regular offensive center will be the best man. (2) Don't limit the candidates to only those who step forward and volunteer. (3) Make sure the player selected for the job can perform under pressure.

Since the extra point snap requires that the ball be centered 7 yards instead of snapped directly into the hands of the quarterback, the regular offensive center may not be as skilled at this task as some other team members. Line up all team members on the 3-yard line and have each one snap several times to a holder located on the 10-yard line. Do not look for perfection, but look instead for the player who makes the ball *zip* back to the holder. (This need not take much time from the practice schedule. Line up as many snappers and holders as there are footballs and have all coaches stand behind the holders, looking for consistently good snaps.) Once the best prospects have been selected they all should be coached on the fundamentals of snapping, such as how to grip the ball and where to snap it so the holder can best catch it. Before making the final selection, test all players under live conditions. Poise and confidence must rate high on the list of qualifications for the snapping job. Once the snapper is found he must be allowed to snap each day, just as a quarterback must be allowed to throw each day, if he is to master this skill.

THE HOLDER

Few players are more underrated than the holder for extra points. Like the offensive lineman, he is seldom noticed until he makes a mistake.

As a general rule, we like to have a quarterback for the holder. Quarterbacks have good hands and are used to pressure. They have experience in controlling the team, and we feel the holder must control the extra point team. The quarterback has, more than likely, just marched the offensive team to a touchdown, handling the football on every play, and should be the best-prepared man to handle the all important extra point snap. Pass receivers also make good holders as they have good hands and are used to keeping their eyes on the ball at all times.

The holder must kneel on one knee, making sure he isn't too close to the kicking tee. His hands should be extended over the tee so the football can be quickly placed in position after it is caught. After catching the ball it must be placed properly on the tee. Most kickers will prefer that it be placed toward the rear of the tee. After the football has been placed on the tee, it should be rotated so that the laces are away from the kicker. This can be easily learned with practice, and once learned takes only a fraction of a second.

One of the main jobs of the holder is to be sure all other extra point team members are set in their positions before the ball is snapped. The holder should first check the offensive linemen and backfield blockers near the line of scrimmage. Once they are set, the holder looks for a nod from the kicker indicating he is ready. He then calls "Down" or "Set." After this call, it is left up to the snapper to snap when he feels ready.

The holder must always be ready for a bad snap. When it occurs, an alternate plan of scoring must be put into effect. Figure 6-1 illustrates a snap that has been centered high over the holder's head. The holder becomes a blocker and the kicker retrieves the ball. The holder calls "Pass" and the two ends and blocking backs release into the end zone as pass receivers.

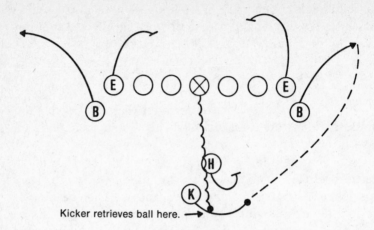

Kicker retrieves ball here. →

FIGURE 6-1

THE KICKER

The extra point kicker must be a dedicated football player who is willing to work on his specialty. Having a strong leg isn't enough. He must develop his steps and timing to perfection.

Most kickers use steps very similar to those in Figure 6-2. The following points are valuable to the kicker:

1. Do not be in too big a hurry to kick. Make sure the holder has had time to place the football squarely on the tee.
2. Remember—on extra points *distance* isn't important, but height is. Kick the ball high by having the toe make contact with the ball as shown in Figure 6-3.
3. Use the same steps each time a kick is made.
4. Be sure to follow through after the kick. Avoid "punching" at the ball.
5. Strike the football with a smooth, steady swing of the leg and foot. Avoid trying to kick the ball out of the park.
6. Like the holder, be ready for a bad snap.

CHOOSING THE EXTRA POINT TEAM

Any coach, if given the football on the 3-yard line and told to score in one play, would certainly choose his most capable and dependable players. This must be done on the extra point specialty

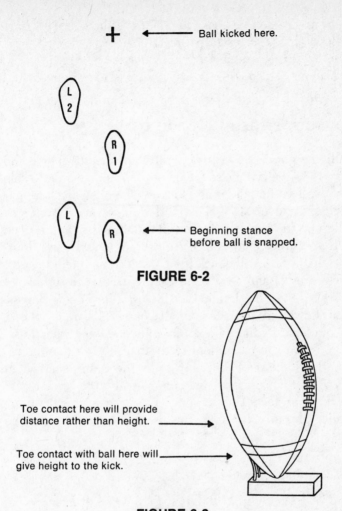

Ball kicked here.

Beginning stance
before ball is snapped.

FIGURE 6-2

Toe contact here will provide
distance rather than height.

Toe contact with ball here will
give height to the kick.

FIGURE 6-3

team. It is a golden opportunity to add one (or two) points to the
score, and this opportunity must not be trusted to untested
players. It is our thought that the regular offensive team, with the
exception of a kicker, holder or snapper, should make up the extra
point team. The regulars more than likely have brought the ball
down the field and scored the touchdown. They should be the
team's best blockers and should possess poise and confidence.
However, some coaches may prefer to insert large players into the
lineup due to the nature of close-order blocking that is used for the

extra point. If defenders cannot penetrate the offensive line, they will seldom block an extra point. If a team is blessed with extra linemen who are good blockers, they may be placed at the blocking back positions. Of course, no player should ever be removed from the extra point team to be rested!

BLOCKING FOR THE EXTRA POINT

The members of the extra point team should align as shown in Figure 6-4. There will be seven offensive linemen and two blocking backs as well as the holder and kicker. The offensive linemen must not take splits over six inches, and some coaches prefer to have them line up toe to toe with no splits at all. After the linemen have taken their three-point stance (some teams will use a four-point stance), the holder will check to be certain the linemen and blocking backs are set and ready. He then checks with the kicker, and when he is ready the holder says "Down" or "Set." The snapper must be allowed to snap the football *when he is ready*, not on a snap count command by the holder. Therefore, the blockers must begin their blocks on the movement of the ball, rather than on a verbal command. (**Note:** We feel that if we let the center snap when he is ready rather than upon verbal command by the holder, the snap will be more perfect. The snapper will have a chance to observe the defenders who are sure to be in his area and snap when he feels comfortable.)

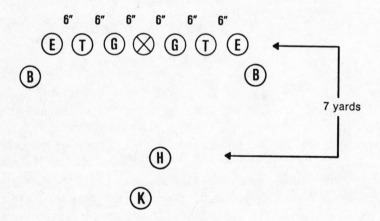

FIGURE 6-4

Once the ball is snapped the offensive linemen take a short jab step to the inside, throwing the head and shoulders across the inside gap, sealing that area against penetration by a defender. Offensive linemen must never pick out a certain defender and block him. They must always block the area, or gap, to their inside. The two blocking backs seal the gap to their inside, near the offensive end. The blocking backs have a fraction of a second longer to observe the rush pattern of the defense than the offensive linemen do. Therefore, if the blocking backs are certain no defender is penetrating the gap to their inside they may block to their outside if a defender should rush in that area.

One warning note for blockers on the extra point team: The defenders may jump around more than usual in an attempt to distract the snapper and kicker. Be still, and do not be drawn offsides. Watch the movement of the ball. Remember, blockers, that you do *not* have to *fire out* after a defender, only seal a gap.

SNAPPING AND KICKING UNDER PRESSURE

Following is a drill to condition the snapper to center the ball to the holder under pressure (see Figure 6-5):

1. Place snapper and holder 7 yards apart. Place three defenders as shown in the diagram (one head-on, one to the left and one to the right of the snapper).

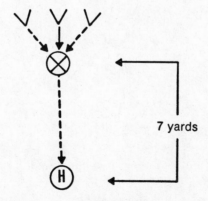

7 yards

FIGURE 6-5

2. Before the snap, let the defenders attempt to rattle the snapper by moving around in the area of the football.

3. After the snap any *one*, or a combination of *two* defenders, charges through the snapper towards the holder. This will condition the snapper to the type of contact he can expect in a game. Occasionally, instruct the defenders not to touch the snapper at all after the snap.

(*Coaching point*: Use this same drill for snappers for punts.)

After doing this drill several times, place two guards beside the center as shown in Figure 6-6. The two guards and snapper are to block the three defenders as they charge the holder and kicker. As the kicker gets used to kicking under this pressure, increase the number of defenders and blockers until the entire defense is rushing the entire extra point team.

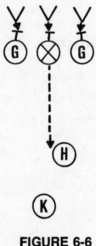

FIGURE 6-6

THE FAKE EXTRA POINT

Figures 6-7 and 6-8 show two slightly different versions of a fake extra point followed by a pass or run option. In Figure 6-7 the holder takes the snap and the kicker becomes a blocker. In Figure 6-8 the roles are exchanged. The routes of the end and blocking

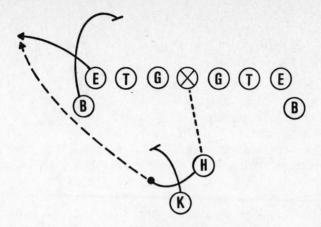

FIGURE 6-7

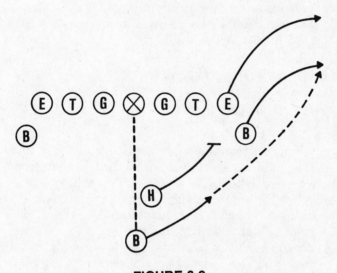

FIGURE 6-8

back can be changed to take best advantage of the defense. Linemen should block as they would for a kick attempt.

When using the fake extra point, the person handling the ball, whether it be the holder or the kicker, must be taught to *run* for the score rather than pass if possible. Although the receiver may be open and the pass thrown softly, there is the possibility the football could be dropped.

WHEN TO KICK FOR ONE POINT

The following rules will help determine when to use the kick following a touchdown:

1. Use the kick if your team scores first. This forces the opposition to make a decision to kick and tie, or to go for two points *if* they score. Also, if the run or pass is tried and fails, the opposition can win with an extra point kick.
2. Use the kick as long as your team is ahead, provided a successful kick will leave your team ahead by at least three points. This forces the opposition to go for a touchdown rather than a field goal in order to beat you.
3. Use the kick when your offensive team has had extreme difficulty during the game moving the ball against the opponent's goal line (or short-yardage) defense.
4. Use the kick when comfortably ahead. Do not show the fake extra point play to your future opponents. You may need it later in the season.

WHEN TO TRY FOR TWO POINTS

Try to run or pass for a two-point conversion in these situations:

1. Whenever two points are needed to *tie* or *go ahead*.
2. When a previous extra point kick has been missed and your team needs to "make up" for the lost point.
3. When the opposition has been successful in previous games in blocking kicks. The fake kick, then run or pass for two points, might surprise them.
4. When your team scores quickly in the early minutes of the game and you wish to demoralize the opposition by getting two points on the conversion. This sudden 8 to 0 lead means the opposition cannot beat you with one score. They must get one touchdown *and* a field goal *or* a second touchdown to win (or three field goals).
5. When the extra point kicker is injured and the ability of the offensive team to make a two-point conversion is greater than the ability of the second team kicker.
6. If weather conditions do not offer a good chance for a successful snap by the center or a good placement of the ball by the holder.

7

The Extra Point Defense
Special Team

WHY THIS TEAM IS NECESSARY

Probably not one coach in ten makes preparations for an extra point defense specialty team. Here is why we feel one is needed and could make the difference between a win and a loss:

1. If it makes sense to spend a great amount of practice time working on making your own extra points, it also should make sense to spend an equal amount of time preparing to defense the opponent's extra point attempt. If this team prevents one extra point that wins one game over the course of the season, it will more than justify its existence.

2. The regular defense may not contain the best-qualified people to rush the kick. Some regular defensive people may be large and rather slow in some positions. Fast, agile players are needed to successfully put pressure on the kicker.

3. The touchdown by the opponent may have been scored on a goal line defensive team. The goal line defense will probably contain even more large and perhaps slower players than the regular defense. Again we need to get these players replaced by quick, agile defenders.

4. After being scored on the regular, or goal line, defenders may feel discouraged. It may be hard for them to put on an all-out rush on the kicker as they may feel they have already failed.

Players with new enthusiasm are needed. These players can come in the form of an extra point defense specialty team.

5. This team provides still another way to get more squad members involved in the game and give them a chance to play an important role in the outcome of the game. Every team has several players who are too small or not talented enough to play as a regular on offense or defense. The only requirements for the extra point defense special team are enthusiasm and hustle plus a little speed or quickness.

WHAT TO BE PREPARED FOR

If the extra point kick is attempted, it is the responsibility of the defensive team to try to block it. The attempted block must be done with design (described later in this chapter). There is no substitution for aggressiveness and quickness if the kick is attempted. The defenders must be fresh and alert and move at the instant the football is snapped.

If a bad snap is made and the ball goes past the holder and kicker, the defenders must react in two ways. Some (6-8 players) must rush in an attempt to recover the football or tackle the offensive player who picks it up. The remaining players should be near the goal line or in the end zone in case the ball is retrieved and a run or pass attempt is made.

If the snap from center is mishandled by the holder, the defensive players will have a fraction of a second longer to get in position to block the kick or to prevent the football from being kicked at all. **Caution**: Do not charge into the holder or kicker (especially after the kick is made) in a manner that will result in a roughing penalty.

If a fake kick followed by a run is attempted, the defenders must not be caught unaware. As the defenders make their charge across the line of scrimmage they must do so in a full-speed manner, but at the same time be alert for the run. Several players must always be placed in the defense to watch especially for the run. For example, players rushing from the outside must always keep the football to their inside. Should the holder, kicker, or other offensive player attempt to take the ball around end, the outside rusher must keep outside leverage and turn the ball carrier back to the inside. **Note:** If the offensive team is noted for their fake kick and run, a change in extra point defense specialty team personnel might be needed. Stronger linemen might be needed in order to discourage a run up the middle.

If a fake kick followed by a pass is attempted, the defenders must be prepared to render a sound pass rush, keeping the passer (probably the holder or the kicker) to their inside. Other defenders will play man-to-man pass defense. All specialty team defensive backs' must know their man-to-man assignment before the ball is snapped. With the defensive backs stress the fact that they may watch their man for half a season with no fake kick and pass being attempted, but they *must* be ready and have their man covered *every time* to insure being protected *when* that one time comes that the offense uses the pass!

If the opposition does not line up in an extra point kick formation the defensive team must be prepared to jump into a goal line defense. If the opposition is known to line up in this manner often and go for two points, the specialty team must be sure to contain enough strength to prevent the easy score from the 3-yard line. If the specialty team personnel is not prepared physically to stop a successful run or pass attempt, *time out* should be called by the defense. The coach may wish to put his goal line defense back into the game.

All of the previously mentioned possibilities should prove the need for having enthusiastic, alert players on the extra point defense specialty team. Convince them of their importance and expect them to become proficient at their task.

BLOCKING THE EXTRA POINT ATTEMPT

Figure 7-1 illustrates an up-the-middle extra point block attempt. Place two of the strongest and most aggressive defensive players at angles toward the outside of the offensive guards as shown in the diagram. Hopefully these players will be stronger than the offensive guards, although this isn't absolutely necessary. On the snap of the ball their job is to drive towards the outside of the offensive guards in an attempt to make the offensive guards block them rather than block an area to their inside as is usually done in extra point blocking. If these defensive linemen do their job, one (or both) of the linebackers should have an open alley up

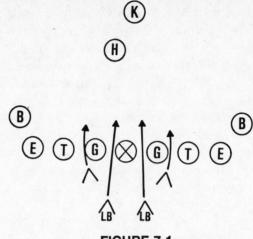

FIGURE 7-1

the middle, with only the block of the center to guard against. Since the center can only block one man the other linebacker should have a clear shot at the block attempt. If only *one* defensive lineman is successful in getting the guard to block him rather than block inside, the play may still work.

Figure 7-2 shows an outside block attempt. Players #1 are to rush the outside shoulder of the blocking backs. If the backs do not block them they are to charge towards a spot in front of the kicking tee in an effort to block the kick. If they are blocked by the backs

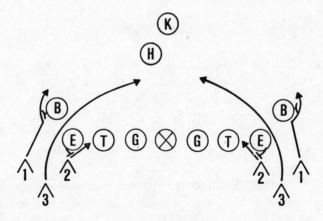

FIGURE 7-2

they are to work to the outside (see diagram), making sure the blocking backs maintain contact with them. Players #2 are to line up head-on the offensive ends and charge to the inside, forcing the ends to block them. Players #3 should be quick and aggressive. They are to fire through the opening created by the blocks of the blocking backs and the ends on Players #1 and 2. Remember: Do not try to block the kick by heading directly for the tee. Head instead for a spot slightly in front of the tee. This will enable the defender to deflect the ball after it has been kicked.

8

The Field Goal
Special Team

THE FIELD GOAL SNAPPER

The center, or snapper, for the field goal attempt will in most instances be the same player who snaps for extra points. It may not be the regular offensive center. The coaches should select the snapper after giving all players (backs, ends, tackles, etc.) an opportunity to demonstrate their snapping ability. Look for the player who can make a sharp, crisp snap with consistent accuracy. Once the top several prospects are selected, allow them to snap under pressure. There is a difference in snapping when the defense is putting on a hard rush up the middle. The snapper must have great poise and confidence. Plan time in every day's schedule to allow the snapper to work on his specialty. When snapping in a game, let him center the football when he feels ready rather than on a snap count from the holder.

THE FIELD GOAL HOLDER

Quarterbacks and receivers usually make the best holders for field goal attempts because of their ability to handle and catch a football. Test these players in practice for quickness in catching the ball and placing it squarely on the kicking tee. Have the holder rotate the football after it is placed on the tee so that the laces are facing the goalpost. This will help to insure that the kicker does not hit the laces, causing the football to go to the right or left rather than straight ahead. Be sure the holder does not kneel too close to the tee, making the kicker feel uncomfortable. Teach the holder to check all offensive linemen and blockers to be sure they are set before indicating to the snapper that he is ready to receive the ball.

THE FIELD GOAL KICKER

It is a mistake for the coach to assume that the extra point kicker will also be the field goal kicker. Some players are very accurate when kicking an extra point, but do not have the leg strength needed for longer kicks, or the ability to kick from an angle. Look first for the kicker who consistently gets *distance* from his kicks. Once this player is found, practice will improve his accuracy.

Make sure the field goal kicker warms up properly before attempting long kicks. He should start from extra point distance and work his way back slowly.

Make sure the kicker uses the same pattern of steps for each kick. Do not destroy the timing between the snapper, the holder, and the kicker, regardless of the length of the kick.

A good follow-through is necessary for maximum kicking distance. Stress this especially with younger kickers.

Remember that a strong leg together with good timing will provide distance for a kick. Never try to "kill the ball" when kicking a field goal.

Always be ready for a bad snap. Do not expect it, but be ready if it should come.

Practice kicking from every possible field position where a field goal might be attempted. Work from the left and right sides of the field. Learn to allow for wind direction when kicking. The kicker should not waste time kicking from distances out of his range.

In practice, kick under pressure at every opportunity. The kicker should feel he has a capable snapper and holder, plus blockers who will provide plenty of time for him to get his kick away

CHOOSING THE FIELD GOAL TEAM

This should be a relatively easy task. The same players who have been chosen for the extra point team will, in most cases, be members of the field goal team. Many coaches prefer to have their regular offensive linemen on the extra point and field goal teams because of their poise and proven athletic ability. Other coaches choose larger linemen who might be better able to cut off the penetration of defensive linemen. Keep in mind that if the field goal is short, or is blocked, and the opponent catches it and attempts a return, there must be players with enough speed and mobility to make the tackle.

PRACTICING THE FIELD GOAL

We feel that the field goal should be practiced in three stages:

1. Provide the kicker with a snapper, a holder, and several managers to catch the kicks. The kicker should start kicking from extra point distance in the center of the field. After successfully making these, the group moves to the left side of the field, then the right side, still kicking from the same distance. Then move the group back to the center of the field, move the ball back five yards, and repeat the process. Continue this pattern, moving the football back five yards each time, until the kicker has reached his maximum kicking range.

2. Place the entire kicking team, plus an 11-man defense, on the field. At the snap let the offensive linemen move into blocking position. Follow step 1, moving the ball left and right, and move the ball five yards farther from the goal post each time.

3. Repeat the step-2 process with the offense blocking and the defense rushing *full speed*.

BLOCKING FOR THE FIELD GOAL

Blocking for a field goal attempt is the same as blocking for an extra point. Read "Blocking for the Extra Point" in Chapter 6. This will explain the same formation and blocking techniques to be used by the field goal team. Remember that blocking for the field goal attempt requires that the offensive linemen *seal* an area to their inside. They are never to fire out, attempting to drive a defender off the line of scrimmage. Remember too that the center should be allowed to snap the football when he is ready and feels comfortable rather than on the holder's command.

It is possible that the field goal team may not feel as much pressure from the defense as the extra point team does. This is because the defense has a larger area to cover when a field goal is being attempted, due to the fact that the line of scrimmage may be the 15- or 20-yard line rather than the 3 as on an extra point attempt. The defense may feel that the possibility of a fake field goal is greater than a fake extra point and therefore not rush as many players.

COVERING DOWNFIELD AFTER THE KICK

There is one major coaching point for members of the field goal team: Unlike the extra point, the field goal attempt that falls short or is kicked off to the side can be picked up and returned by the defensive team. Therefore, after the kick all members of the field goal team must quickly fan out and sprint downfield to protect against a possible return (see Figure 8-1). Players must be *drilled to cover after the kick*. It is a natural tendency to block, then stop and watch the ball to see if it clears the goalposts.

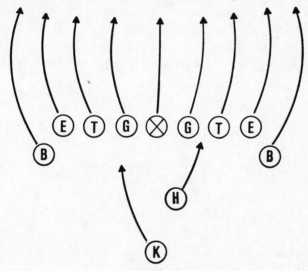

FIGURE 8-1

SNAPPING AND KICKING UNDER PRESSURE

Kicking field goals under pressure in a game is like any other phase of football. Its success will be in direct proportion to the

amount of time spent kicking under pressure in practice. The
snapper, holder, and kicker, as well as the offensive linemen, must
have the feeling they have "done this before" each time they line
up for a field goal attempt in a game. The drills shown in Figures
6-5 and 6-6 in Chapter Six will help to develop a field goal team
that can perform under pressure.

THE FAKE FIELD GOAL

Figures 6-7 and 6-8 in Chapter Six illustrate ways to fake a
field goal and go for the first down or the touchdown. Figure 8-2
shows still another way to gain yardage on the fake field goal.
(**Note:** Holder should hold the football momentarily in order to
"draw the defenders to the inside," making it easier to run around
them.) The biggest difference to keep in mind when attempting the
fake field goal is that on the fake extra point only 3 yards is needed,
while on a fake field goal there is usually need for more yardage.
Also keep in mind where the ball will be located if the fake field
goal should fail to gain sufficient first-down (or touchdown) yardage. **Example:** The football is on the 18-yard line and the offense
needs to get to the 12-yard line for a first down. A fake field goal is
attempted but gains only 4 yards. The ball will be turned over to

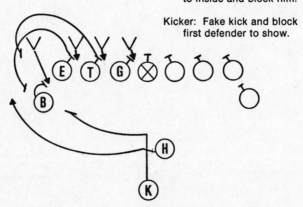

LE and LT: Bump defender to
   inside and release.

Left Blocking Back: Draw defender
   to inside and block him.

Kicker: Fake kick and block
   first defender to show.

FIGURE 8-2

the opponents on the 14-yard line. A missed field goal attempt would have brought the ball to the 20. There is a field position gain of 6 yards although the fake field goal attempt failed to make the first down.

MOVING THE BALL INTO FIELD GOAL POSITION

There are three factors involved in moving the football into field goal position:

1. Get the football as near the goal as possible.
2. Get the football as near the center of the field as possible.
3. Consider the range of the kicker. (One kicker will have a reasonable chance of success if the ball gets to the 20-yard line—a 37-yard field goal, while another kicker won't have much chance of making the kick unless the ball is snapped from the 10-yard line—a 27-yard field goal.)

As the ball is being driven into field goal range the following points should be kept in mind:

1. Avoid risky passes that might be intercepted.
2. Remember that an incomplete pass wastes a down and will not move the ball any closer to the goal. Use short, safe passes.
3. Never use plays that could possibly lose big yardage, such as deep reverses or risky option plays where a wild pitch might occur.
4. Be especially careful of penalties that can take the offense out of field goal range.
5. Consider any weather conditions, such as wind or rain, that can lengthen or shorten the range of the field goal kicker.

POSITIONING THE BALL IN FRONT OF THE GOALPOST

Once the football has been moved into field goal range, it must be positioned squarely in front of the goalpost. This enables the kicker to view the goalpost as a *wide* target area rather than as a much smaller target area as seen from an angle.

All players, especially the quarterback, running backs, and receivers, should know ways to keep the ball positioned in front of the goalpost. Plays must be called directing the point of attack toward the center of the field. Ball carriers must avoid going out-of-bounds, which would result in the ball being put into play at the hash mark. Pass receivers should run routes in the middle of the field rather than sideline routes.

The closer the offensive team gets to the yard line where a field goal might be attempted, the safer the play selection should be. Quarterback sneaks and up-the-middle fullback drives seldom, if ever, lose yardage and the chance of a fumble is slight.

Once the football is safely in field goal position and in easy range of the kicker, it is good strategy to go ahead and kick on second or third down rather than waiting until fourth down. This is especially true late in the game when a field goal will win the game and there is no need to drive for a touchdown. A kick on second or third down eliminates the risk of a fumble by a ball carrier. Should the snap be fumbled by the field goal holder, the ball could be recovered and another attempt made on the next down.

9

The Onside Kick
Special Team

WHEN TO ONSIDE KICK

There are at least five situations where you might consider using an onside kick:

1. Use the onside kick *as a surprise move*. Since most teams do not use the onside kick often, the receiving team may be totally unprepared. Use scouting reports to determine the exact location of each receiving team member. Also try to determine the mental alertness of receiving team members. (Do front line players communicate and seem to be warning their teammates of the possibility of an onside kick, or do the receiving team players methodically take the field in an unsuspecting manner?)

2. Use the onside kick *against a strong team*. When facing a team with superior personnel your team may need a break to stay in the game. A successfully executed onside kick, at the beginning of the game or at the start of the second half, could supply the spark needed for an upset.

3. Use the onside kick *against a weak team*. If it works it could lead to a quick touchdown and demoralize your opponent. If it fails your defense still has a good chance to contain this weak opponent.

4. Use the onside kick *when the momentum of the game is swinging your way*. This is one the best times to use the onside kick because it is seldom expected by the receiving team. For example,

assume your team and your opponent have played a scoreless game and it is early in the fourth quarter. Your opponent is driving for a touchdown and is on your 15-yard line when your safety man intercepts a pass in the flats and returns it 85 yards for the game's first touchdown. Discouraged by their failure to score and your team's great defensive play, your opponent will not expect an onside kick. If the kick is successful and your team regains possession of the football, your team would be in excellent position to control the remainder of the game.

5. Use the onside kick *late in the game* when your team is behind and must have the football. **Example**: Trailing 7-0, your team scores but misses the extra point and still trails 7-6. There are only 55 seconds left in the game and ball possession is your only hope for victory. Of course, this is the most difficult time to execute the onside kick successfully as your opponent will be looking for it and will probably place at least seven or eight players near the front receiving line.

TYPE OF PLAYERS NEEDED

All players on the *regular* kickoff team should be the squad's fastest, most aggressive, and surest tackling players. Therefore, there should be little reason to alternate personnel for the onside kick specialty team. There is one exception. The coach might prefer to place the *five best* of the 11 kickoff team players all on one side of the football and kick the ball in that direction (see Figure 9-1). We feel that most receiving teams would never notice this slight alteration of players. All players on the onside kick team must be willing to work to perfect their specialty. The coach must sell them on the idea that one successfully recovered onside kick can mean the difference between a win or a loss.

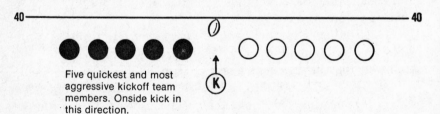

Five quickest and most aggressive kickoff team members. Onside kick in this direction.

FIGURE 9-1

BLOCKING OPPONENTS IN THE KICK AREA

The first step in recovering an onside kick is to make sure the opposing team doesn't recover it. This is the primary job of two of the onside kick specialty team members. Figure 9-2 illustrates an onside kick team with five players on each side of the football. In this illustration the ball will be kicked to the left side, so the five quickest defenders are placed on the left side. Two of these players are to block two members of the receiving team, preventing them from recovering the football. The other three players are to head directly for the football, as shown in the diagram. The two players designated to block the receiving team members must be disciplined athletes. It will be a temptation to go after the ball. These two players are to sprint directly towards the two front line players, as shown in the diagram. If one of the front line receiving team players is attempting to catch the football, these players are to tackle him quickly, aiming their shoulders at the football in an effort to cause a fumble. Remember that these front line players are seldom coached in the art of handling and protecting the football.

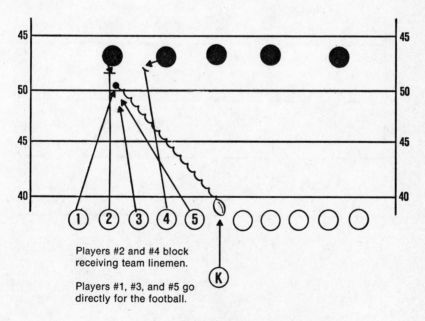

Players #2 and #4 block receiving team linemen.

Players #1, #3, and #5 go directly for the football.

FIGURE 9-2

If the ball is kicked accurately, the kicking team should be able to outnumber the receiving team in the area of the football by 5 to 2 (see Figure 9-3).

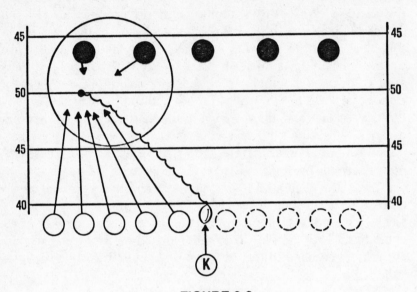

FIGURE 9-3

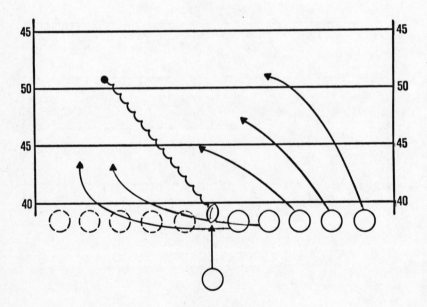

FIGURE 9-4

Coaching point: The five players located on the opposite side of the field from the direction of the onside kick must not go downfield as usual. They should take pursuit angles as shown in Figure 9-4. The job of these players is very important, for if the onside kick isn't successful there must be players in position to prevent a long return.

THE ONSIDE KICK

Here are points to remember when teaching the onside kick:

1. The kicker should begin his approach to the football from the same distance as he does for a regular long kickoff.
2. Begin the approach at the same speed as for a regular long kickoff.
3. As the kicker nears the football he should slow down slightly and bring himself under control.
4. The toe should hit the football higher up on the ball than usual. This will prevent the ball from being kicked softly into the air where it could be handled easily. It should cause the ball to bounce or roll along the ground where it will be more difficult to catch. Remember, we plan to have five players in the recovery area to our opponent's two.
5. No onside kick can be legally recovered by the kicking team until it has gone the required 10 yards. Make sure the ball is kicked with enough power to drive it 10 yards.
6. Avoid kicking the football on the extreme outside edge. This often causes the ball to spin and prevents it from carrying 10 yards.
7. Onside kick team members must remember that the onside kicker will slow down slightly as he nears the football. They must not be offsides by crossing the 40-yard line before the football has been kicked.

THE CROSS-FIELD KICK

Another way to onside kick is shown in Figure 9-5. Six players should be located on one side of the ball and four on the other, with the kicker in the middle. As the ball is kicked, players #2 and #4 are to block receiving team players A and B. Players #1, #3, #5, and #6 go for the football. **Note**: Some coaches may prefer to let player #6 block receiving team player C as shown in Figure 9-6.

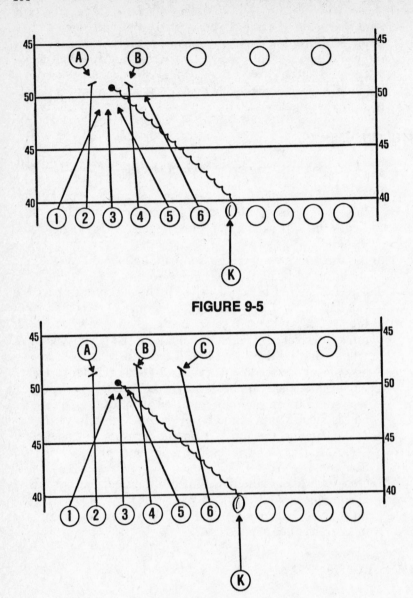

FIGURE 9-5

FIGURE 9-6

Figure 9-7 illustrates a surprise onside kick executed by a player other than the normal kickoff man. Player A places the football on the tee, takes his position, listens for the referee's whistle, and begins his approach to the football. When he gets approximately 3 yards from the football he stops. Player B, who is positioned about 4 yards from the ball, steps quickly at a 45-degree angle and kicks the ball. Some coaches will prefer the regular low-to-the-ground bouncing type of kick. Others may want the football kicked soft and high (like a lazy extra point attempt). The height of the ball allows the six recovery men time to cross the 50-yard line before the ball lands. *Remember, however, that the ball cannot be touched by the kicking team players until it has hit the ground.*

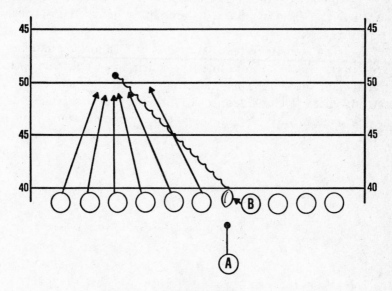

FIGURE 9-7

ERRORS TO PREVENT WHEN ONSIDE KICKING

1. Prevent offsides penalties. In their eagerness to recover the football, players are more likely to cross their own 40-yard line before the ball is kicked. Few things are more discouraging than successfully recovering an onside kick only to have a penalty nullify the play.

2. Make sure the kick goes over 10 yards. Allow the kicker to practice onside kicks at every opportunity so that he can get the feel of kicking the necessary distance. Make sure players know not to touch the football until it has gone the required distance.

3. Do not use the onside kick too often. The best chance to recover an onside kick is to have an unsuspecting receiving team.

4. Avoid any unusual huddling, talking, or movement prior to the onside kick that might alert the receiving team of a possible onside kick attempt.

5. Do not always onside kick to the same side (right or left). Locate the opposing team's front line players who seem to have the slowest reactions and kick toward them. The kicker should practice every day kicking to his right and to his left.

6. Do not kick the football out of bounds by kicking it too hard toward the sideline, as this will completely defeat the purpose of the onside kick.

7. If the receiving team suspects an onside kick and brings extra players near the front line, the coach may want to change his strategy and kick long. This can be indicated to the kicking team by your signal from the sideline just prior to the kick. The onside kicking team must be taught to look for such a signal.

10

The Onside Kick-
Receiving Special Team

WHEN TO EXPECT AN ONSIDE KICK

Look for an onside kick in the following situations:

1. Early in the game, as a suprise move. Previous scouting reports should be consulted to see if the opponent has ever used the onside kick to start the game.
2. After a long, sudden touchdown play by the opponent. Returning an intercepted pass, running a punt back, or making a long run from scrimmage for a touchdown might inspire the opposition to try to gain firm control of the game by recovering an onside kick.
3. If the opponent is the underdog and will need to take risks in order to pull an upset.
4. If the momentum of the game is swinging in favor of the opposition.
5. If the opposing coach has been known to use the onside kick on occasion.
6. Late in the game when the opposition is trailing. This is the most likely time to expect an onside kick.

TYPE OF PLAYERS NEEDED

The onside kick-receiving special team should be used any time there is good reason to expect an onside kick attempt. Special personnel will be needed for this team. There is no place here for slow reacting players. Look for these qualities when selecting members of the onside kick receiving team:

1. *Good hands* on players, especially those who will be positioned on the front line.
2. *Quickness*, which enables players to get to the football.
3. *Aggressiveness*, needed in warding off block attempts and battling opponents for the ball.
4. *Intelligence*, to watch for any unusual alignment of kickoff team players that could indicate an onside attempt, or to judge whether to handle a kick near the sideline or to let it go out of bounds.

COACHING THE ONSIDE KICK-RECEIVING TEAM

Explain to the onside kick-receiving team the ways the kicking team will possibly attempt to recover their own kick. Show them how several players will be assigned the job of blocking receiving team members away from the football while other kicking team players go directly for the football (see Chapter 9). Use the drill shown in Figure 10-1 to prepare receiving team players for the onside kick. Place a kicker and four kick-off team players as shown in the illustration. Place a front line receiving team player opposite each kicking team player. The kicker may onside kick to either side. (**Note:** If he kicks to his left side the players on his right side are inactive.) One kickoff team player blocks one receiving team player while the two remaining players go for the football as shown in the diagram.

Here are some points to stress to players who will be receiving an onside kick:

1. Unless the football is kicked directly into your hands do not try to run with it. There will not be time for any blocking pattern to be set up by your teammates. Also, the chance of a fumble would be great.
2. Get the football as soon as possible. Fall on it and protect it. Cover the football firmly with the hands and arms. Cradle the ball with as much of the body as possible to prevent it from being knocked loose.
3. Never wait for the ball, expecting it to bounce right into your hands. You must pursue the football aggressively.

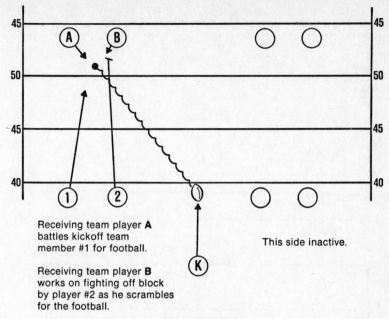

Receiving team player **A** battles kickoff team member #1 for football.

This side inactive.

Receiving team player **B** works on fighting off block by player #2 as he scrambles for the football.

FIGURE 10-1

4. Be prepared for a block by a kickoff team player in an attempt to keep you away from the football.
5. Be prepared to block for a teammate if the kick should be long and caught by one of the deep backs.
6. Use good judgment if the football is kicked hard toward the sideline. It is often better to allow the ball to go out of bounds untouched (it still belongs to the receiving team) than to risk mishandling it.
7. Some kickers may kick the ball low and hard directly at a front line player, hoping that a fumble will result when he tries to catch it. Be ready for this. It is better to let the ball go past and be handled by another player than to fumble it back to the kicking team.

LINING UP TO DEFENSE THE ONSIDE KICK

Figure 10-2 shows the lineup for an onside kick-receiving team. There are two waves of players set to receive the kick, five on the front line and four behind them. This formation provides for at least five receiving team players in the recovery area regardless of where the ball is kicked (see Figure 10-3).

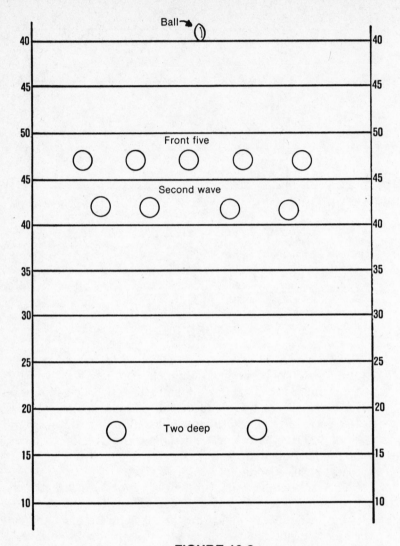

FIGURE 10-2

If the ball is kicked long, the front five players are to block the first kickoff players down the field. The second wave of four players will drop back, wait for the ball to be caught, and lead the ball carrier up the middle.

There are several slightly different ways to position players who are expecting an onside kick. However, always be sure to keep at least two players deep in case the football is kicked long.

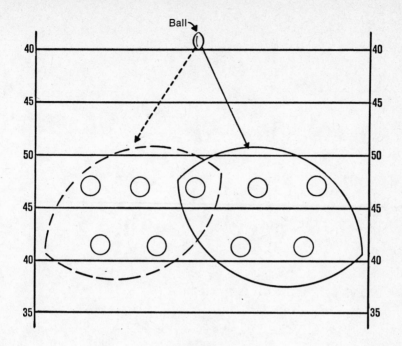

FIGURE 10-3

11

The Quick Kick
Special Team

REASONS FOR QUICK KICKING

There are two general differences between a quick kick and a regular punt. The quick kick is executed suddenly and without warning, and it originates from a regular offensive formation rather than from the normal punt formation. The quick kick is an excellent offensive weapon. When used successfully it can provide outstanding field position for the kicking team.

There are several reasons for installing the quick kick. First, it is very effective against a team that has an outstanding punt-return team featuring excellent broken field runners. There should be no return yardage after a quick kick. Even if the ball is fielded, there will be no blocking pattern, or wall, set up for the ball carrier. Second, the quick kick should be used against defensive teams that are noted for their fourth down punt-rushing ability. Since the quick kick comes as a surprise move (usually on third down), the defensive team will not be sending eight or nine players at the kicker in attempt to block the kick. Third, the quick kick can cover up for an inadequate snapper (one who has difficulty making the 10-14 yard snap to a punter in a regular punt formation). Of course, a team can't use the quick kick each time it desires to punt the football, but it will help take some of the pressure off a poor snapper.

Some coaches will argue that the quick kick "isn't used much anymore." Maybe this is true. But why shouldn't your team avail itself of this potentially dangerous weapon? If it helps win one football game a season it will be well worth the time and effort spent teaching it.

WHEN TO QUICK KICK

Consider a quick kick in the following situations:

1. When facing a team that might not know how to react to a quick kick. (Some teams see quick kicks so seldom that they tend to stand and watch after the kick, unsure of what they should do or whom they should block.)
2. When there is a strong wind to your back, which would carry the football far beyond the defensive safety man.
3. When the defensive team is jamming your offense by playing their secondary defenders near the line of scrimmage.
4. When you have a strong defensive team that you know can contain your opponents.
5. When your opponents have a strong defensive team and your offense is unable to move consistently. (Quick kick the football to them and play for a break.)
6. As a psychological move to swing the momentum of the game to your team.
7. When the weather is bad (rain and wind), and the snapper is having a difficult time making successful snaps to the punter.
8. On any third down, when the defense is not thinking about receiving a punted ball.
9. When your offense is backed up deep in its own territory and is having trouble making yards.
10. When your regular punter (if he is not the same player as the one who quick kicks) is injured and his replacement is not adequate.
11. When you do not want to give the receiving team time to set up a planned return wall.

WHEN NEVER TO QUICK KICK

There are certain times when the quick kick should never be used:

1. Never quick kick until the players on the quick kick team have perfected their assignments. Make sure all blocking assignments are known. Be sure the backfield play has been thoroughly taught. Be certain all players know their coverage patterns after the football has been kicked.
2. Never quick kick unless you have a good quick *kicker*. Test the kicker under pressure in practice many times before allowing him to quick kick in a game.
3. Never quick kick when playing a great offensive team that will probably gain yardage easily against your defense.
4. Never quick kick *into* a high wind.
5. Do not use the quick kick on fourth down. It will not be a surprise and will be totally ineffective. (There could be one exception to this. Let's say you are playing a team with a reputation for returning punts. You are on their 45-yard line, fourth and one. Line up in a regular offensive formation as if to run a play trying for the first down. If the opponent pulls its entire defense—safety men and all—up close to stop the fourth-down try, use the quick kick from the regular offensive formation. If the defensive safety men do not come up, call time out, go back in the huddle, and call for the regular punt formation.)
6. Never use the quick kick on third down *only*. Opponents will learn to look for it. Occasionally use second down.
7. Never quick kick when trailing late in the game. You might not get the football back again.

COACHING THE KICKER

Find a player with a strong leg and kicking experience (if possible), who is willing to work on his specialty, likes the thrill of an exciting play, and will not panic under pressure, and you've got your potential quick kicker. After showing him the basic play, teach him the mechanics of the quick kick itself (the play design will be described later in this chapter).

The right-footed quick kicker (reverse steps for a left-footed kicker) should be positioned at the left halfback or fullback position. On the snap of the ball he takes a step with his right foot at a 45-degree angle away from the line of scrimmage (see Figure 11-1). He should receive the football from the quarterback as his right foot touches the ground. He then steps with his left foot and at the

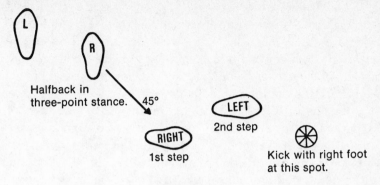

FIGURE 11-1

same time positions the football parallel to his body, holding one end of the football with each hand. After stepping with the left foot he kicks the football, making sure the foot makes contact with the ball in the area of the white stripe on the right side of the ball (see Figure 11-2). Contact with the football at this point will cause the ball to travel end-over-end, giving it a continuous bounce toward the opponent's goal once it hits the ground. After completing his follow-through, the kicker starts his kick coverage pattern.

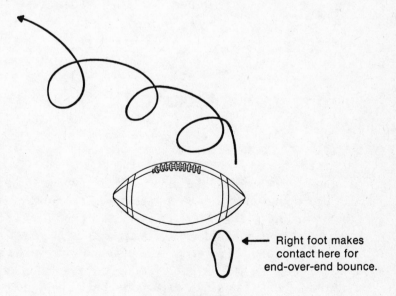

FIGURE 11-2

Allow the kicker to develop his pattern of steps and learn to get a good roll from his end-over-end kick before making him kick under pressure. When he is ready to kick under pressure, work him into it slowly to build his confidence. Place a center, quarterback, quick kicker, and one defensive player on the field as shown in Figure 11-3. Let the one defender rush the kick over the center while the center works on blocking him. Gradually add two offensive guards and two defenders over them, then two offensive tackles and two more defenders, etc. until the *entire* offensive and defensive teams are practicing this play. Remember, when practicing the quick kick under pressure, that the defenders (in practice) are looking for the quick kick and are trying to block it. This will not be the case in a real game as the kick will come as a surprise move.

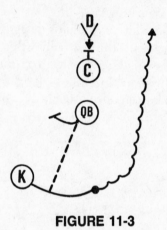

FIGURE 11-3

QUICK KICK TEAM PERSONNEL

The quick kick team will be one special team where there will be very little opportunity to make a large number of substitutions. Bringing in several (4-7) players for a quick kick team would obviously alert the opponent's defensive players and the quick kick would lose the element of surprise. It would almost assure the play of failure. Therefore, it is imperative that the regular offensive team also serve as the quick kick specialty team. The one exception, of course, is the kicker.

It is almost necessary to select a quick kicker who is a running back. If a guard or tackle is selected, he could easily be noticed as he lines up in the quick kicker's halfback or fullback position. His jersey number (in the 60's or 70's) would easily give him away. Since most backs are generally good athletes it should not be too difficult to find one to do the job. Make sure the back lines up at the quick kick position (left back or fullback for a right-footed kicker) several times during the game even though this might not be his normal backfield position (he might be a slot back or flanker). By doing this he will not look conspicuous when he lines up at the halfback or fullback position for the purpose of executing the quick kick.

Other than the kicker, no other changes in personnel are required. However, if you have, for example, two right tackles, one big and slow and the other smaller and faster, be sure the fastest player is inserted into the game several plays before the quick kick. His speed will be useful covering the kick.

EXECUTING THE QUICK KICK

The basic backfield fundamentals for the quick kick will remain the same regardless of the style of offense used. Therefore the quick kick is easily adaptable to your present offensive plans.

Quarterback. The quarterback takes his normal stance behind the center. After receiving the snap he opens to his left side (for a right-footed kicker) and steps towards the kicker with his left foot. The direction of his step will vary slightly depending on whether the kicker is lined up at left halfback or at fullback. He tosses the football to the kicker in a soft, easy-to-catch manner. After getting rid of the ball the quarterback steps back to his right with the right foot and blocks any defender who might have broken through the left side of the offensive line.

Kicker. The kicker must be lined up at left halfback or fullback (right halfback or fullback for left-footed kicker). After the snap of the ball he steps and kicks as explained previously in this chapter in "Coaching the Kicker."

Other Two Backs. Of the two remaining backs, one should be positioned in a running back position (fullback or right halfback) while the other can be a wingback or slotback or wide flanker. Or, if you prefer, both remaining backs can be placed in the running back positions. One of these two backs must be placed in the backfield to the right of the kicker. (**Examples:** if the kicker is at left halfback, place one back at fullback *or* right halfback. If the kicker is at fullback, place one back at right halfback.) As soon as the ball is snapped to the quarterback this back is to take two steps to the right, in the direction of the defensive end. He then turns to his right and circles behind the kicker, checking for a fumbled toss from the quarterback or for a blocked kick. If neither has occurred, he follows his kick coverage pattern.

The *one remaining back* is used primarily to cover the kick. If he is lined up at wingback or slotback he will block before covering the kick. If he is positioned as a wide receiver or as a third running back, he covers the kick with no blocking assignment.

The following diagrams show how the quick kick can be run from a wide variety of formations. Figure 11-4 shows a *Wing-T* formation. The left halfback kicks and the fullback checks for the fumble or a blocked kick. Figure 11-5 shows the wingback on the left side and the fullback kicking while the right halfback checks.

Figure 11-6 shows a *Pro-I* formation with the fullback kicking and the tailback checking. The roles are reversed in Figure 11-7 as the tailback kicks and the fullback checks.

Figure 11-8 illustrates a *divided* style of backfield quick kick. This may be the easiest type of formation to kick from as there is good distance between the halfbacks and therefore it does not crowd the kicker.

Figure 11-9, the *Wishbone* formation, and Figure 11-10, the *Straight-T* formation, are similar in that the three running backs are basically side by side. In both of these formations the left halfback is the kicker, the fullback is the check man, and the right halfback sprints immediately downfield to cover the kick.

If the *Power-I* formation is used there are a variety of ways to execute the quick kick. Figure 11-11 shows a Power-I Right formation with the *fullback kicking*, the tailback checking and the right halfback covering the kick. Figure 11-12 shows the *tailback kicking* while the fullback checks and the right halfback covers. By shifting to a Power-Left as shown in Figure 11-13 the *left halfback* can kick with the fullback covering and the tailback checking. The Power-I coach, by using all three methods of quick kicking, should be able to keep opponents guessing as to when a quick kick is coming.

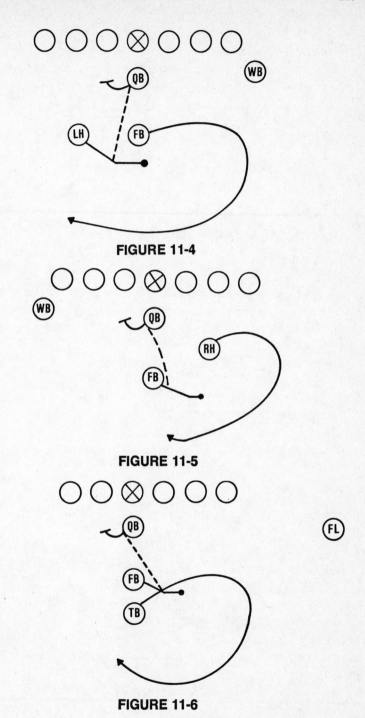

FIGURE 11-4

FIGURE 11-5

FIGURE 11-6

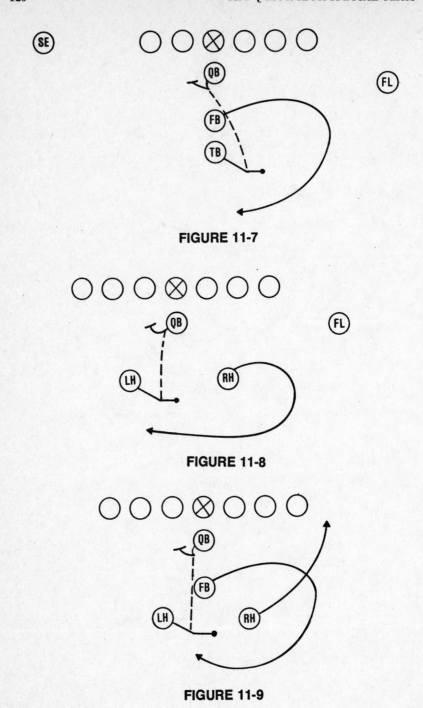

FIGURE 11-7

FIGURE 11-8

FIGURE 11-9

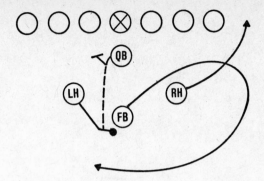

FIGURE 11-10

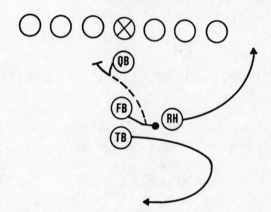

FIGURE 11-11

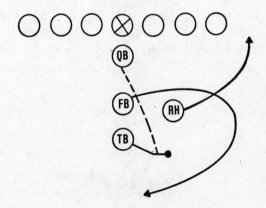

FIGURE 11-12

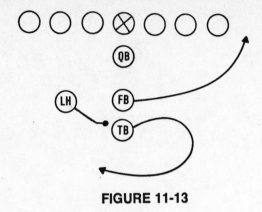

FIGURE 11-13

BLOCKING FOR THE QUICK KICK

Regardless of the offensive formation used, the football will be kicked in the area shown in Figure 11-14. Therefore, this area must be given priority in blocking protection. The blocking rule for linemen is this: *Seal the inside gap.* Unless this area is protected completely there is the possibility the kick could be blocked. Any tight wingback or slotback should follow the same blocking rule as the offensive linemen. Figure 11-15 shows the offensive linemen and a wingback sealing the inside gap and cutting off any penetration by the defense. Those blocking on the line of scrimmage should fire out hard and *low*, shooting at the lower part of the defensive player's legs. This should force the defender to keep his hands low in an effort to ward off the block. With the defender's hands low there will be little chance of a blocked kick.

FIGURE 11-14

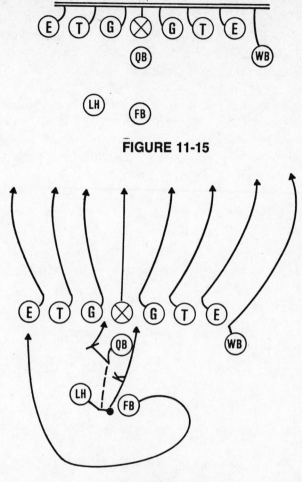

FIGURE 11-15

FIGURE 11-16

COVERING THE QUICK KICK

After making their blocks and the football has been kicked, all players must immediately scramble to their feet and sprint downfield. If the ball has not been handled, they must surround it, allowing it to continue rolling as long as it is rolling in the direction of the opponent's goal. Should the ball bounce back in the direction it was kicked, the players must immediately down it.

If a defensive safety man has handled the kick and has started a return, the coverage team must remember the rules for covering any kick: (1) sprint downfield, staying in lanes; (2) come under control as they near the ball carrier; (3) never let the ball carrier get around the defenders to the outside; and (4) never try to make a tackle around the ankles, especially if the return back is small and shifty.

Quick kick team members must be drilled daily on the exact paths they are to take in covering the quick kick. Figure 11-16 illustrates quick kick coverage from a wing-T formation. Slight adjustments will be necessary, depending on the type of offensive formation used by the kicking team.

12

The Goal Line Stand
Special Team

PERSONNEL

The goal line stand defensive team, perhaps more than any other special team, must be selected with extreme care. This is no place to experiment with untested or unproven players. It is no place to insert a young player with little experience. A mistake by a defensive player near the goal line will probably result in an offensive score. Here are some guidelines to use in selecting the goal line special team:

1. Select the *top eleven defensive players*, regardless of any attempts to use a two-platoon offensive and defensive system. The squad's best defensive athletes must be on the field with no exceptions!

2. Select players who are *mentally tough*. This refers to players who think they cannot be scored on by any team. Seniors with experience are generally the leaders here. They are older and often stronger physically than the other squad members. Confidence, without cockiness, is a trademark of a mentally tough player.

3. Select players who are *physically tough*. Near the goal line the opponent's offensive team will be using plenty of hard-hitting, straight-ahead plays. These plays call for double-team and wedge

blocking and the defensive players must be physically strong enough to hold their ground.

4. Select players who are the *best competitors* on the team. Some players naturally like to compete when the pressure is greatest. These players are often described simply as "winners" by their coaches. They will usually find some way to come up with the big play and prevent a score.

5. Select players who are *coachable*. Each goal line defensive player must execute his position techniques exactly as they were taught to him by his coach. A mistake by a defensive player allowing the ball carrier an additional few feet, or even inches, could result in a score.

6. Get as much *quickness* as possible into the lineup. By quickness we do not necessarily mean speed. Near the goal line there is a greater need for the player who has quick reactions within a small confined area than for the player who has "100-yard dash" speed. Plenty of big men have this quickness although they have only average speed.

7. Get as much *size* as possible in the lineup. However, *size must never be substituted for any of the six other characteristics*. All other characteristics being equal, a 6'2", 230-pound, defensive player will be harder to move out of the way than a 5'11" 165-pound player.

WHAT TO EXPECT FROM OPPONENTS ON THE GOAL LINE

It is a serious coaching mistake to allow the goal line stand specialty team to play a game without knowledge of what to expect from the offensive team when inside the 10-yard line. The play selection of the offensive team will depend on the number of the down plus the exact location of the football inside the 10-yard line. For example, if the ball is on the 9-yard line, first and goal to go, the offensive team will probably need one big play of 4 or 5 yards to get the ball across the goal. Four straight quarterback sneaks probably won't be enough to get the six points. More wide-open plays will be tried. However, if the ball is on the 2-yard line, first and goal to go, it would be reasonable to look for several short-yardage plays such as quarterback sneaks or quick fullback dive plays. The goal line defense specialty team must always be aware of down and distance inside the 10-yard line. After judging the play tendencies based on the down and distance to the goal line, the defenders should also consider these points:

1. *What have been the offensive team's best (most successful) plays throughout the season?* The offensive team certainly isn't going to try unproven plays inside the 10-yard line. It is quite reasonable to assume they will select one of their top five or six offensive plays. This narrows their list of potential goal line plays to a workable few. If the defensive coach has studied the scouting reports of his offensive opponent he should know what these plays are.

> (*Coaching point*: It is for this reason that your scout must not just bring back a diagram of the plays used by the offensive team, but must also indicate which plays were used in goal line situations.)

2.*What have been the offensive team's most successful plays in this game?* As the game progresses the offensive strategy of your opponent will become evident. Their strategy will be based on your style of defense, your defensive personnel, and weather conditions, plus the score of the game. Although goal line offensive plays are sometimes different from "middle of the field" plays, it should not be too difficult to establish a general pattern of basic plays that the offensive team has designed for your defense. Many offensive teams, when near the goal line, will use the "we'll dance with the one who brung us" philosophy. That is, they will continue to use the same plays near the goal line that were successful in getting them to their opponent's 10-yard line.

3. *Where are your weakest defensive players located?* Just as your staff knows plenty about your opponent's offensive and defensive plans, rest assured that your opponent knows plenty about your defensive personnel. They know where your weakest links are and what their defensive responsibilities are, and, of course, this is where they will probably attack. This can be used to your advantage. Moving players around (for example, moving the weak left defensive tackle to right tackle and filling the left tackle spot with a strong defensive player) might cancel any advantage the offense

might have had over the defensive team. At any rate, knowing the strengths—and especially the weaknesses—of your own team may give a clue as to where the offensive team will strike.

4. *Expect power plays near the goal line*. Since the defense will have 11 men near the line of scrimmage, the offense must fight strength with strength and use their best power plays near the goal line. Plays such as the *isolation* (or *lead*) play (Figure 12-1) provide double team blocking at the point of attack. A wing back and end crossblock adds power for the fullback off-tackle play as shown in Figure 12-2. A quarterback keep play (see Figure 12-3) provides plenty of power blocking in front of the quarterback as he sweeps for the corner of the goal line. Figures 12-4 and 12-5 illustrate two other power plays often used inside the 10-yard line.

5. *Expect the best back to carry the football near the goal line*. Near the goal, it is safe to say that the offense will run their best back at least 50 percent (if not 75 or even 100 percent) of the time. This fact should be drilled into the defensive team players, but not to the extent that they overlook other ball carriers. Some offensive teams will attempt to score by faking with the best back and handing instead to the least likely candidate. However, as a general rule, watch for the best back in the tough situations.

6. *Look for wedge blocking near the goal line*. Wedge blocking consists of several offensive linemen driving into an area, shoulder to shoulder, with no particular defensive men to block. It can be very effective, especially near the goal line where individual blocking assignments often get confused with the change in defenses. Figure 12-6 shows the fullback driving straight ahead behind wedge blocking up the middle. Wedge blocking is very difficult to defend against, especially if the offensive linemen are big and strong and get off the ball quickly.

7. *Expect limited ball handling near the goal line*. Unless the offensive team is noted for using the option play (where a pitch is part of the play), look for plays where the quarterback can safely handle the football without taking chances on a fumble by himself or the back carrying the ball. Plays where the quarterback simply takes the snap and hands the football directly to the ball carrier without faking can be expected.

8. *No need to worry about the long pass play*. Once an offensive team gets inside the 10-yard line they have *less* than 20 yards

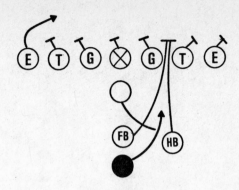

FIGURE 12-1

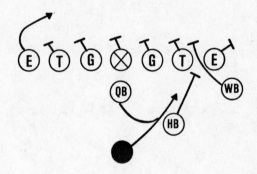

FIGURE 12-2

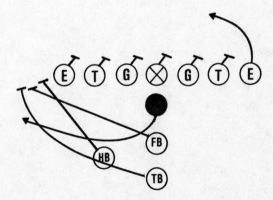

FIGURE 12-3

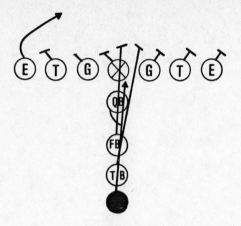

FIGURE 12-4

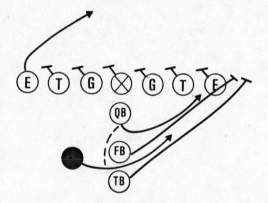

FIGURE 12-5

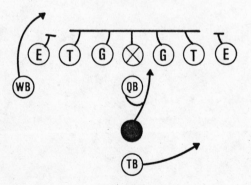

FIGURE 12-6

in which to operate their offense (10 yards in the end zone, plus the yardage between the 10 and the goal line). Therefore, the defensive team has no worry about the *long* pass play. This eliminates one phase of the offense and enables the defense to concentrate on other areas of attack.

9. *Do not expect reverses or other plays that develop deep in the offensive team's backfield.* Once inside the 10-yard line, most offensive teams are reluctant to try plays that could result in an offensive back being caught several yards deep in the backfield. Although the reverse play shown in Figure 12-7 is a fine play, most offensive teams will not take the risk of losing 4 or 5 yards on it. Goal line stand defensive players should look first for the quick-hitting play. Quick-hitting plays seldom lose yardage and therefore never leave the offensive team in worse field position than before the play began.

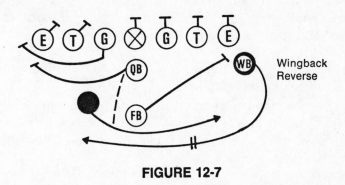

FIGURE 12-7

10. *Be prepared for quick passes.* Although many coaches consider passing risky, it is often the best (and only) way to get the ball across the goal line. Let's face it. Goal line defensive teams are usually tough. The offensive team knows this. If they try once or twice and fail to advance the ball on the ground, it certainly makes sense to look for the pass. As stated earlier, only short passes can be attempted near the goal line due to the limited space (yardage to the goal line, plus 10 yards of end zone). Most offensive teams won't have more than two or three consistently good short passes. Know what they are, and if the running game fails, look for one of them.

11. *Expect the quarterback to call for the snap after a reason-*

ably short snap count. A good quarterback will not risk having his team jump offsides by calling a long, drawn-out snap count. Losing 5 yards for an offsides penalty inside the 10-yard line would be a serious error.

In summary, a smart goal line stand defensive team can gain an advantage over the offense by knowing what plays to expect near the goal line and what plays probably won't be used. After making adjustments based on this knowledge, any goal line defensive team should be able to do a better job protecting its end zone.

GOAL LINE DEFENSES

Although you may have your own personal style of goal line defense, there are three goal line defenses that are used by most teams. They are the 6-5, the Gap-8, and the 7-4.

The 6-5 defense is shown in Figure 12-8. It is a very sound defense, combining a strong running defense with good pass protection. The basic techniques of the defense are as follows:

Ends: Line up a yard outside the offensive end. Drive across the line of scrimmage through the offensive side of the off-tackle hole. If met by a backfield blocker, try to drive through him and destroy his block. Do not avoid the block by going around the blocker. Never "box" or play "soft," creating a hole in the off-tackle area.

Tackles: Line up head-on the offensive tackle. Drive to the inside gap. Get penetration but never penetrate deeper than the football. (**Note:** Some teams prefer to line the tackle up on the outside shoulder of the offensive tackle and drive through the offensive tackle toward the inside gap.)

Guards: Line up in the guard-center gap. On the snap of the ball drive low and hard through the gap, getting penetration. Grab the legs or arms of the quarterback as quickly as possible. Be careful not to penetrate straight ahead *ignoring* the quarterback and allowing him to dive between the two defensive guards for good yardage (see Figure 12-9).

Middle Linebacker: This man is the key to the success of the 6-5 defense. By all means station the best, most aggressive linebacker

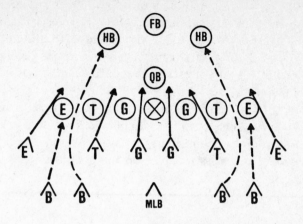

6-5 defense

– – – – – – – indicates man-to-man pass coverage.

FIGURE 12-8

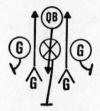

FIGURE 12-9

at this spot. His job is to locate the football and go to it. His immediate responsibility is to help stop any ball carrier who runs inside the offensive tackles. Although size isn't the main requirement for this position, it helps, especially since the offensive team will use many power plays as well as wedge blocking near the goal line.

Defensive Backs: There will be four of these players in the lineup. Some coaches may not call them all defensive backs (they may call one or two of them linebackers). Regardlesss of the terminology used, all four will be called on to play pass defense on occasion. The two *outside* defensive backs will cover the *widest* eligible pass receivers on their side, using man-to-man coverage. The two *inside* defensive backs will cover the *second widest* receivers on their side, using man-to-man coverage. These backs must play near the

line of scrimmage and cover their men as closely as possible. *The
closer the offensive team gets to the goal line, the closer the defensive backs play to the line of scrimmage.* Under no circumstance
should a defensive back position himself 5 or 6 yards deep in the
end zone. Once the receiver catches the football and steps into the
end zone it's all over!

Figure 12-10 illustrates the proper man-to-man pass coverage
against the wing-T offense with two eligible pass receivers on each
side of the center. If the scouting report indicates that the fullback
is sometimes used as a pass receiver on the goal line, the middle
linebacker could be assigned to cover him.

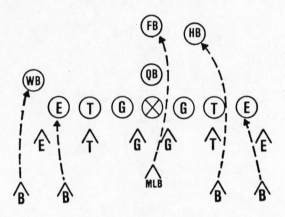

Man-to-man vs. Wing-T offense.

FIGURE 12-10

Figure 12-11 shows the man-to-man coverage of an offense
using a wide flanker, a slit end and the I formation. Assign the
middle linebacker to the fullback if he is a pass-receiving threat.

Figure 12-12 shows an offense with *three* eligible receivers all
on the same side of the football. As shown in the diagram, three
defensive backs must move to the same side in order to match up
the man-to-man coverage. Middle linebacker takes the fullback if
there is reason to suspect him of being a pass receiver.

The Gap-8 defense (see Figure 12-13) is perhaps the most
commonly used goal line defense. It is relatively simple to teach.
As shown in the diagram, eight players are positioned in the offen-

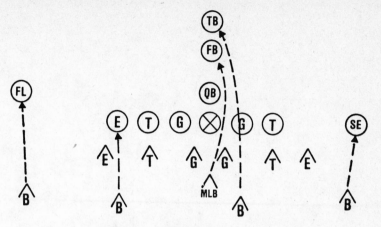

Man-to-man coverage vs. I formation.

FIGURE 12-11

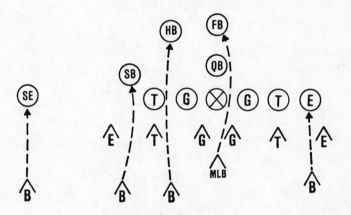

Man-to-man coverage vs. three eligible receivers on one side.

FIGURE 12-12

sive gaps. The two inside players nearest the offensive center are to charge low and hard through the gap. They must make every effort to get to the quarterback before he can execute his play. If he attempts to hand off, these two defensive players should try to grab his hands or arms and cause him to fumble or make a bad handoff to his running back. These players can often knock the quarterback's

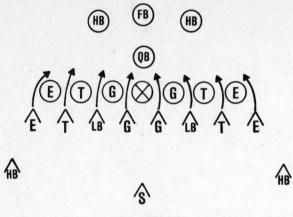

Gap-8 defense

FIGURE 12-13

legs from under him as he pulls out to move down the line of scrimmage for a handoff or a quarterback keep play.

The four defenders lined up in the guard-tackle gaps and the tackle-end gaps must penetrate low and hard across the line and react to the football.

The defensive ends line up 1-1½ yards outside the offensive ends. They should be in a three-point stance (some coaches may prefer the two-point stance) and ready to fire into the backfield. If a dropback pass develops, the ends should rush hard, making sure they keep the quarterback to their inside. If the ball goes away, the end will serve as trail man watching for a reverse. The ends must not "box" or allow themselves to be blocked "out." This would create a large hole in the off-tackle area.

The two outside halfbacks position themselves slightly outside the defensive ends. They key the offensive ends. If the ends release, the halfbacks must drop back and play pass defense in their area. If the offensive end blocks down, the halfback must come up to the outside and turn the running play back to the inside.

The middle safety man lines up directly over the offensive center. His depth will depend on the distance between the football and the goal line. If the football is on the 8-yard line, the middle safety might be 7 or 8 yards deep. If the football is on the 2-yard

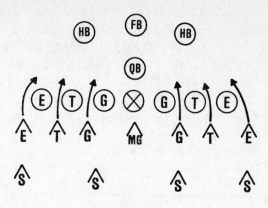

7-4 Defense

FIGURE 12-14

line he will be only 2 or 3 yards deep. The middle safety should read the blocks of the offensive linemen to determine if the play is a pass or run. If a run develops, the safety man must move laterally along the line of scrimmage, positioning himself to help make the tackle. If a pass is indicated, he must drop back, watching any receiver coming into the middle area.

Figure 12-14 shows the 7-4 goal line defense. We feel this defense is most effective when the offense is on the 6-, 7-, 8- or 9-yard line rather than on the 1- through 5-yard lines. As you can see in the diagram there is no defensive player penetrating the gaps inside the offensive guards. This makes the defense vulnerable to quick plays up the middle, such as the quarterback sneak or the quick fullback drive play, and this is why the defense is not often used inside the 5-yard line.

The ends in the 7-4 alignment play as described in the end play for the Gap-8 defense. They must come hard across the line of scrimmage and not allow themselves to be "kicked out" by a blocking halfback or a pulling guard.

The two tackles line up in the gaps between the offensive ends and offensive tackles. They are to penetrate the gap and react to the football, being careful not to "run past the football" by going too deep.

The two guards are positioned in the offensive guard-tackle

gaps. They must fire through the gaps, reacting to the football. They too must get penetration without "overrunning" the ball.

The defender head-on center is in a four-point stance. He is to charge into the center after the snap of the ball. His goal is to knock the center into the offensive backfield. He must never allow the center to drive him off the line of scrimmage.

The outside safety men line up just outside the offensive ends. If the offensive ends block, they come up to the outside. If the ends release, they drop back and play pass.

The two inside safety men are positioned just outside the offensive guards. Their depth will depend on the yard line the football is on. If the football is on the 2- or 3-yard line, they should be about the same distance (2 or 3 yards) from the ball. If the ball is on the 7-yard line, they will back up to 4 or 5 yards off the ball. These defensive players should key the offensive guards. If they block aggressively, they must watch for the run and be ready to help seal the area between the offensive guards and the center. If the offensive guards pass block, the defenders will drop back to the middle area and play pass defense.

COACHING POINTS WHEN PLAYING GOAL LINE DEFENSE

1. All halfbacks and safety men must be brought up closer to the line of scrimmage than on normal defenses.

2. Whatever the style of defense used, all defensive players on the line of scrimmage must penetrate, or at least hold their ground. They cannot afford to be driven back.

3. All linemen must stay low. The lineman who raises up is giving his opponent a much larger blocking area. Also, a defensive lineman who stands up has little driving power.

4. Use man-to-man pass coverage whenever possible. A zone pass defense has gaps in it. On the goal line it takes only a quick, short, 4- or 5-yard pass to get in the end zone. Zone pass defenders often can't react quickly enough to close this gap.

5. Always go for the football when tackling if possible. A fumble recovery by the defense near their own goal line can change the course of the game.

PRACTICING THE GOAL LINE DEFENSE

It is our belief that many coaches are guilty of not allowing their goal line defense specialty team sufficient practice time. Yet here is where many games are won and lost. It really matters very little how many yards are gained by the opposition in the middle of the field. It does matter whether or not they gain 2 or 3 yards when they are on the goal line. Therefore, we believe each coach must discipline himself to build plenty of practice time for the goal line defense into the practice schedule, taking some of the time from the practice of the regular defense if necessary.

When practicing the goal line defense we believe in having the toughest offensive players possible running against the defense. This is the only sure way to test the goal line defense. If the squad is small in number, and only a few "really tough" players are available, use a *half-line scrimmage* as shown in Figure 12-15. This is done by scrimmaging the left side of the defense against the remainder of the team's toughest players. Then switch over and scrimmage the right side of the defense against the "best of the rest."

Remember to give plenty of praise to the goal line defense for its accomplishments, both in games and in practice. Morale must be high if these players are to perform at their best. Let them know you think *they* will come through even if all else fails!

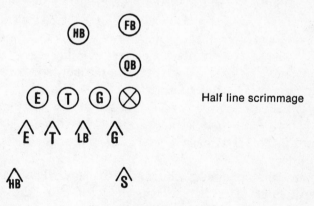

Half line scrimmage

FIGURE 12-15

13

The Goal Line Offense
Special Team

WHY IT IS NEEDED

Like the other special teams, the goal line offensive team has a
very special job—to get the football across the goal line *under the
most severe circumstances*. Defenses will be stacked against them
near the line of scrimmage using nine-, ten-, and eleven-man
fronts. The best defensive players on the opposing team will surely
be in the game. Defensive alignments not usually seen outside the
goal line area will be threatening the offense. For these reasons,
each squad should have a special goal line offensive team. These
players must be coached to block against the Gap-8 defense, the
6-5 defense, the 7-4 defense, and any other goal line defense used
by the opponents.

Failure to score after getting inside the 10-yard line can lead to
defeat. Although many touchdowns are scored from 25, 40, or 60
yards out, no team will win consistently unless it can get the tough
goal line yards a good percentage of the time. Therefore these
players must be selected with extreme care. Along with the goal
line defensive team, the goal line offensive team will probably
decide the outcome of more games than any other special team
used.

PERSONNEL

There are a number of factors to consider when selecting goal line offensive team personnel:

1. Size. 155- to 170-pound offensive linemen will not consistently block 200- to 210-pound defensive players unless the smaller players are unusually strong for their size and the larger players are not as strong as their size would indicate. Any 11-man defensive front (and most goal line defenses could be considered 11-man fronts) will be strong in number and mass even if some individual players are not strong. Therefore, a goal line offensive team must match size with size at as many positions as possible. Most large players can be drilled to fire out straight ahead and block, and to use the gap block (this block will be used often against goal line defenses). The goal line offensive team is a good special team for the larger linemen who aren't proficient at pulling, trapping, or downfield blocking. Train these large players to fire out, make contact, and maintain that contact while driving their feet, and short goal line yardage can usually be obtained.

Many teams like to use large offensive linemen at new positions on the goal line to get as much size in the lineup as possible. One of the simplest moves is to use large substitute tackles at the end positions *if* the offensive ends are small and in the game largely because of their pass-catching ability. Figure 13-1 shows small pass-catching ends replaced by large tackles, giving the offensive line additional size. Figure 13-2 illustrates a large lineman being placed at wingback to provide near the line of scrimmage an *eighth* blocker who has good size. Figure 13-3 shows the large lineman at slotback providing the same benefit.

Figures 13-4 and 13-5 indicate how a large lineman could be utilized at the halfback or fullback position to take advantage of his size in a key blocking position.

2. Strength. Some players are not physically large but have great strength not found in some larger athletes. These men may weigh between 175 and 190 pounds, but because of leg and body strength may be more effective than some 200- to 220-pound players. In

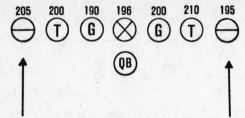

Use large tackles here to replace smaller ends.
Provides additional blocking strength near goal line.

FIGURE 13-1

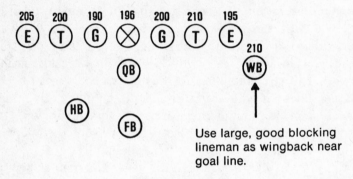

Use large, good blocking
lineman as wingback near
goal line.

FIGURE 13-2

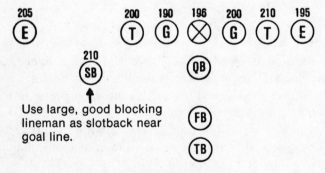

Use large, good blocking
lineman as slotback near
goal line.

FIGURE 13-3

fact, many coaches prefer the strong 185-pound player over the
slower 210-pounder because the smaller player is probably quicker
and can better execute a variety of offensive moves such as trapping.

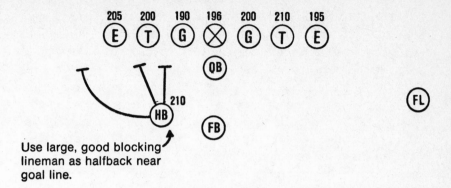

Use large, good blocking
lineman as halfback near
goal line.

FIGURE 13-4

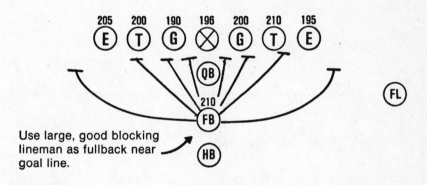

Use large, good blocking
lineman as fullback near
goal line.

FIGURE 13-5

Regardless of the preference of the coach, he must have players with good size *or* excellent strength to consistently move the football inside the 10-yard line against good goal line defensive teams.

3. **Best Back**. We feel that any time the offensive team gets inside the opponent's 10-yard line, the team's best running back (in fact *all* the team's best running backs) must be in the game. Some of these players may have been previously taken out for any number of reasons. Big backs, if available, are good to have in the game near the goal line *if they are tough runners*. But by all means, the squad's top ball carrier must be called on for these crucial plays.

4. Big Receivers. Since speed cannot be used for the purpose of running deep pass patterns on the goal line, it is a good idea to select goal line offensive team receivers on the basis of the size of the target they present to the passing quarterback. A big tall receiver provides this excellent target. On the goal line the passes are short. The receiver needs only to take a few steps across the goal line and turn towards the quarterback, looking for the ball. In the mass confusion of 22 players in the congested goal line area, it is a welcome sight for the quarterback to spot his tall receiver in the end zone. If the tall receiver is matched with a much shorter defensive back, the quarterback can toss the football higher than usual (see Figure 13-6). Of course, make sure the tall receiver has good hands and is competitive enough to fight for the football in these tough scoring situations.

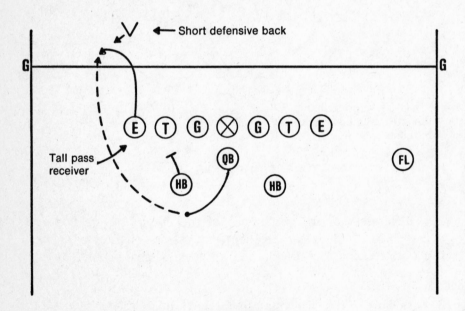

FIGURE 13-6

5. Downfield Blockers. If the football is on the 8- or 9-yard line, downfield blockers are definitely needed. However, when the ball is on the 1- or 2-yard line, any player (such as a split end) who may be used primarily as a downfield blocker may need to be replaced by another blocker who is more proficient at blocking on the line of scrimmage.

PRACTICING THE GOAL LINE OFFENSE

To develop into an effective scoring unit the goal line offense special team must consistently practice against the toughest defensive players possible. If the squad uses the two-platoon system (one group of players for offense and another group for defense), this will be relatively easy to do since the goal line offense could practice against the squad's own goal line defensive team. If the squad is small in number or the two-platoon system isn't used, the offensive team can still practice in sections against the remaining toughest players on the squad. For example, to practice the isolation or lead play up the middle, use only a center, two guards, a quarterback and two running backs (total of six players), against four defensive players (see Figure 13-7). To practice an off-tackle play (see Figure 13-8) all that is needed is a center, quarterback, halfback, fullback, end, and two defensive players (total of seven players).

Since most goal line defensive teams will contain the largest players available, the goal line offensive team must drill against big, hard-to-move defenders. In other words, prepare the goal line offensive team for what they will actually see during a real game situation. Practicing against small, 150-pound, third string players will never develop a strong goal line offensive machine.

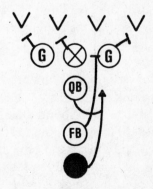

FIGURE 13-7

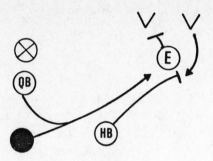

FIGURE 13-8

It is the job of the head coach to build plenty of practice time into the daily practice schedule for the goal line offensive team. We have often found it good for the morale of the players to practice goal line offense at the end of the daily practice. We often give them a certain goal to accomplish while practicing goal line offense. For example, we might require the offense to score three times from the 9-yard line (giving them four downs to make the 9 yards) before ending the day's practice. If the offense fails to score in four downs, the football is brought back to the 9 and the play series started over again. To insure stiff defensive competition we sometimes will cut down on the number of post-practice sprints for the defenders each time they hold the goal line offense scoreless in a four-down series from the 9-yard line.

Although the toughest defensive players available must be used in scrimmage against the goal line offense, the coach must be careful that the offensive team does not lose confidence in its ability to score against a tough defense. Keep in mind that it is extremely hard to score against any goal line defense, due to the 11 defenders jammed near the line of scrimmage. Do not constantly criticize the goal line offensive team unless their failure to score is from a lack of effort. Instead, continue to offer sound coaching and encouragement. Experiment with different plays and move personnel about until the best combination of plays and personnel is being utilized in the goal line scoring effort. Compliment the offensive players when they are successful in scoring. *Confidence* may be the most important weapon of the goal line offense!

GOAL LINE OFFENSE PLAYS

It is best if the goal line offense plays can be selected from the list of regular offensive plays. These plays have been practiced time and again throughout the season as well as used in getting the football into the scoring zone. However, due to the nature of goal line defenses, slight alterations may be necessary. For example, an offense that normally uses two wide receivers and two split running backs, one of whom is often in motion, may have a hard time running off-tackle or up-the-middle plays due to a lack of blockers (see Figure 13-9) in these areas. By bringing the split end in and moving the wide flanker to a tight wingback position, plus eliminating the motion, the blocking possibilities are increased (see Figure 13-10). This does not necessarily mean that motion and wide receivers cannot be effective on the goal line, but it does mean that slight adjustments might have to be made in offensive style near the goal line in order to more effectively run certain plays.

Before deciding which plays are most effective on the goal line, consider those plays which are usually not used near the goal line. Long pass patterns of course can be eliminated first. Reverses, especially inside the 5-yard line, are a gamble. Many teams are reluctant to use a screen or draw play near the goal line. Both could lose big yardage if not successful. However, we have seen both the screen and the draw used near the goal line, and it must be the decision of each coach whether to include these plays in his goal line offense.

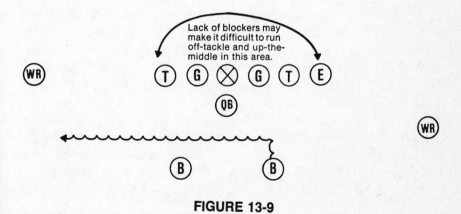

FIGURE 13-9

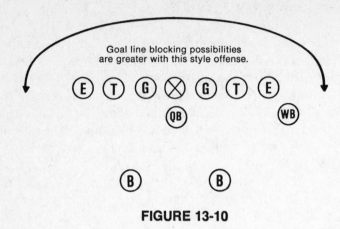

Goal line blocking possibilities
are greater with this style offense.

FIGURE 13-10

In the following diagrams we will illustrate some goal line plays that we have used successfully. Each play will be diagramed against the Gap-8, the 6-5, or the 7-4 defense, depending on the best defense to use that particular play against. Each coach should make slight play adjustments, depending on his style of offense. (**Example:** We might show a trap play from a wing-T formation. Another coach may want to use the same trap play run from his I-formation.)

Figure 13-11 shows a quick *trap* play from a wing-T formation against a Gap-8 defense. Blocking assignments are relatively easy for any trap play against an 8-man line. Figure 13-12 shows the same play against a 7-4 defense.

The same type of *trap* play can be run wider (trap the defensive end) as shown in Figure 13-13 against a Gap-8 defense.

Option plays, as shown in Figure 13-14 against a 6-5 defense and as shown in Figure 13-15 against the Gap-8 defense, are good goal line plays if the quarterback has good judgment and can make an adequate toss to the pitch man if necessary.

The *quick pitch* is a good goal line play against the Gap-8 (Figure 13-16), the 6-5 (Figure 13-17), or the 7-4 (Figure 13-18). In each of the quick pitch play diagrams the end and tackle are both pulling behind the wingback to lead the play. If no wingback is used, pull the tackle, but leave the end to reach block the first man to his outside.

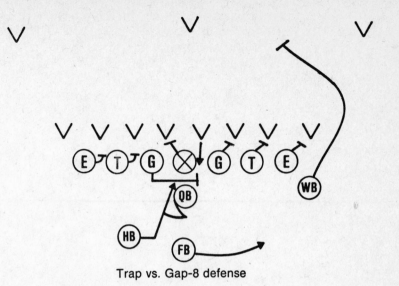

Trap vs. Gap-8 defense

FIGURE 13-11

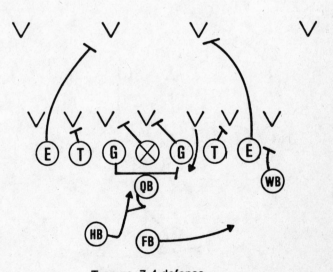

Trap vs. 7-4 defense

FIGURE 13-12

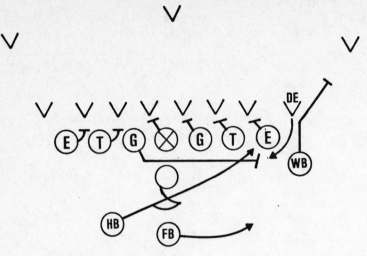

Wide trap vs. Gap-8

FIGURE 13-13

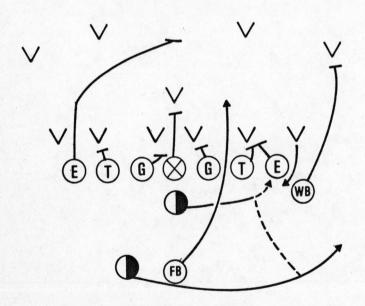

Option play vs. 6-5 defense

FIGURE 13-14

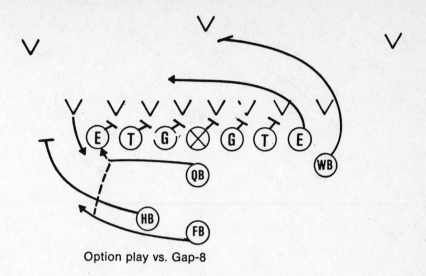

Option play vs. Gap-8

FIGURE 13-15

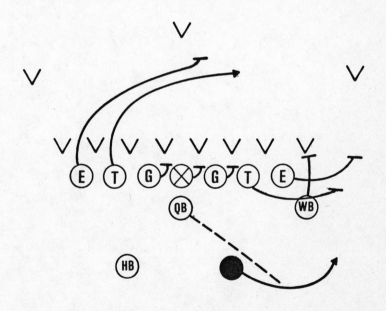

Quick pitch vs. Gap-8

FIGURE 13-16

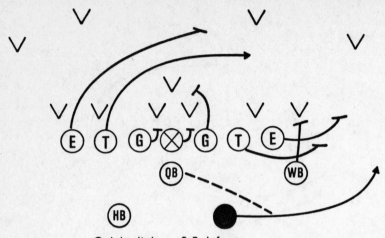

Quick pitch vs. 6-5 defense

FIGURE 13-17

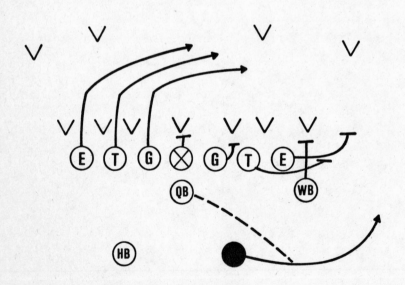

Quick pitch vs. 7-4 defense

FIGURE 13-18

The *isolation* (or *lead*) play is one of the best goal line plays. To run this play well the offensive team must have at least one back who is a strong, tough blocker. We like to run this play directly at a linebacker; however, some goal line defenses do not have a linebacker in the hole where we want to run. Therefore, the back's job is to block anyone in the hole whether he is a linebacker or a down lineman. Against the 7-4 defense, the *Power-I* formation isolation is an excellent choice (see Figure 13-19). Figure 13-20 shows the same play against a 6-5 defense, while Figure 13-21 shows a wing-I formation with only one back blocking the defender in the hole. Figure 13-22 illustrates a one-back isolation block after a crossbuck fake in the backfield.

A fullback or halfback *dive* play can be effective against the 7-4 or the 6-5 defense, especially when short yardage (less than 2 yards) is needed. Figure 13-23 shows a fullback dive play against a 7-4 defense. Figure 13-24 is the halfback dive against a 6-5 defense.

The *quarterback sneak* may be the best of all short-yardage goal line plays. If the center-quarterback exchange is good, there is very little chance of a fumble since the ball isn't handed off to another player. It is almost impossible to lose yardage on this play. In executing this play the quarterback should look over the defensive alignment and find the nearest "open gap." After taking the snap he drives into this "open gap" low and hard. If the defensive players are driving through the gaps low to the ground, the quarterback may want to dive over them. This should be done only when there is extremely short distance (less than a yard) to the goal line. Against a 7-4 defense, the quarterback may sneak behind either guard (see Figure 13-25). Against a Gap-8, driving straight ahead is probably the best route (see Figure 13-26).

Sweeps can be effective near the goal line if the blocking is good. Since sweeps around end take longer to develop than straight-ahead plays, all blockers must hold their blocks longer than on quick-hitting plays up the middle. Figure 13-27 shows an end sweep against a 7-4 defense with both guards pulling. As shown in Figure 13-28, we prefer to pull the offside but not the onside guard when blocking against the Gap-8 defense.

Wedge blocking (all linemen blocking the area to the inside in a close-order, shoulder-to-shoulder fashion) is very effective near the goal against any defense (see Figure 13-29).

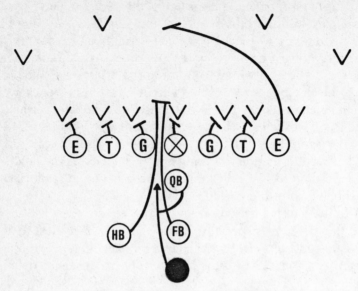

Isolation (lead) play vs. 7-4 defense

FIGURE 13-19

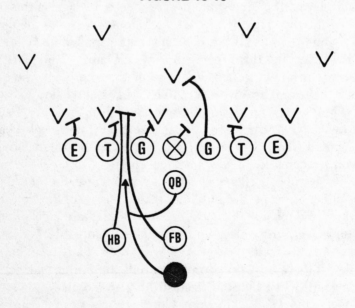

Isolation (lead) play vs. 6-5 defense

FIGURE 13-20

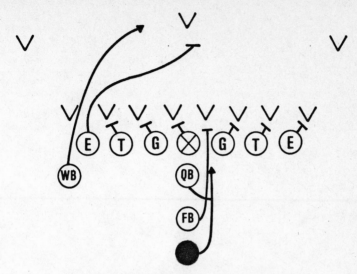

Isolation (lead) play from Wing-I formation

FIGURE 13-21

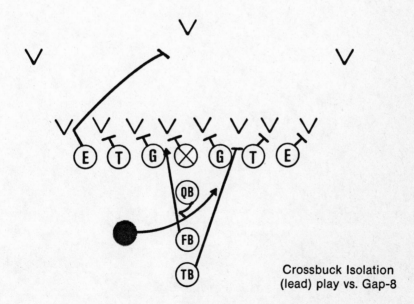

Crossbuck Isolation
(lead) play vs. Gap-8

FIGURE 13-22

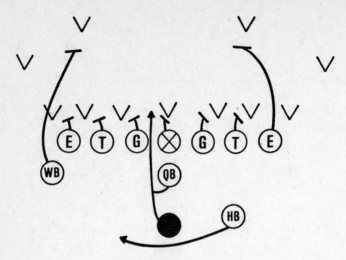

Fullback dive vs. 7-4

FIGURE 13-23

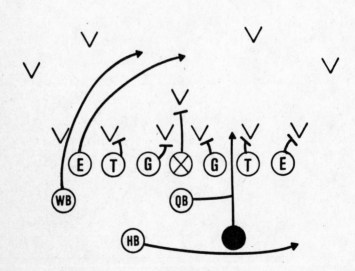

Halfback dive vs. 6-5 defense

FIGURE 13-24

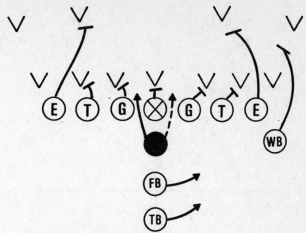

Quarterback sneak behind either guard vs. 7-4

FIGURE 13-25

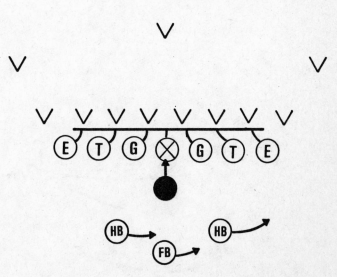

Quarterback sneak vs. Gap-8 (wedge blocking)

FIGURE 13-26

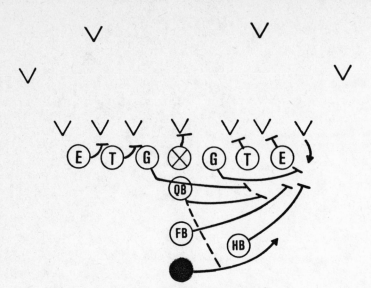

End sweep vs. 7-4 defense. Both guards pulling.

FIGURE 13-27

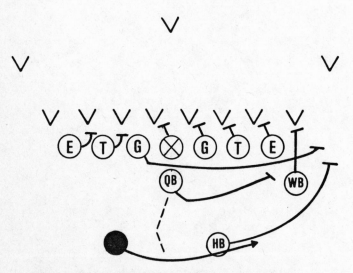

End sweep vs. Gap-8. Only offside guard pulls.

FIGURE 13-28

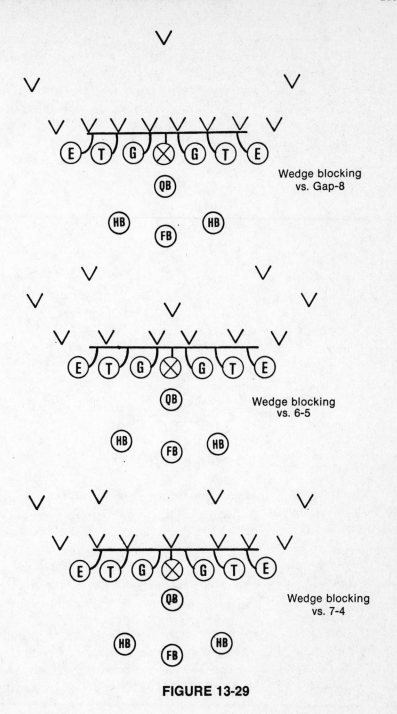

Wedge blocking
vs. Gap-8

Wedge blocking
vs. 6-5

Wedge blocking
vs. 7-4

FIGURE 13-29

Motion can be used to loosen up the tight goal line defense. For example, the play in Figure 13-30 sends the left halfback in motion to the right. The defense will probably cover the flanker and the motion man with one-on-one coverage. The quarterback has the option to pass quickly to the flanker or the man in motion, or to keep the football and sprint for the goal line. This play puts tremendous pressure on the defensive players on the corner of the defense. Also, either tight end can be used in the pass pattern if the coach desires.

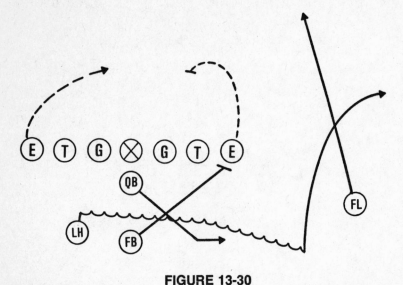

FIGURE 13-30

There are many pass patterns that can be used on the goal line. In the *play action pass* in Figure 13-31, the primary receiver is the left end. He fakes a block to the inside before running his short, quick route.

A *bootleg pass* (Figure 13-32) can often take advantage of an overanxious defense. The backs fake a sweep to the right. The pulling of one or both guards is optional, depending on the defense.

If a halfback is a good passer, use the *quick pitch pass* (Figure 13-33). The quick pitch should draw the defensive backs up to stop what they believe to be a run. (**Note:** If the defensive backs stay back, run the football. Never pass into any defended area near the goal line.)

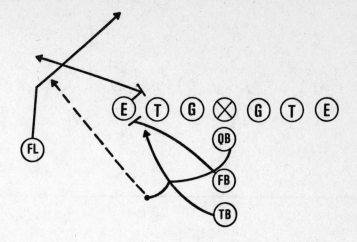

FIGURE 13-31

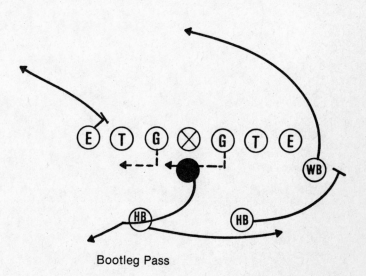

Bootleg Pass

FIGURE 13-32

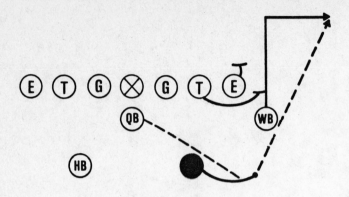

Quick Pitch Pass

FIGURE 13-33

14

The Pass Defense
Special Team

WHEN TO USE IT

Football teams fall into four categories:

1. Teams that use the run almost exclusively and rarely pass.
2. Teams that have an equal balance between the run and the pass.
3. Teams that would rather pass than run.
4. Teams that use the pass almost exclusively and rarely run.

The teams in categories 3 and 4 make the pass defense special team necessary. There are also other situations that call for the use of this team:

1. On second or third down and long yardage for a first down.
2. Late in the half to prevent a pass for a score.
3. Late in a game against a team that likes to run, but must rely on the pass for longer yardage.
4. Against a weak opponent who prefers to run but can't move the football and must rely, hopefully, on completing some passes to move the ball or score.

The pass defense special team must be designed so that it can be inserted into the game quickly and easily when the need arises. Those players selected for this special team must remain near the coach on the sidelines during the entire game. They should be ready to enter the game for one play at a time, or be prepared to play the entire game if necessary.

PERSONNEL

The number of pass defense specialty players who will be inserted into the game during passing situations will vary according to each particular team's style of defense and regular defensive personnel. Some teams may need to replace only one regular defender with a pass defense specialty player. Other teams may replace up to seven or eight regular players.

Members of the pass defense special team will fall into one of two groups: those who *rush the passer* and *contain his movements*, and those who *cover the receivers* and *defend against the pass*.

Those players selected to be on the front line and whose job is to rush and contain the passer can range widely in size. Some coaches will want big strong linemen who can drive past a blocker, using physical strength to get to the quarterback. Other coaches prefer smaller, quicker linemen who can maneuver rapidly into the offensive backfield, putting sudden pressure on the passer. Either style can be very effective. A combination of both styles can be effective. We prefer the smaller, quicker linemen, but this is strictly a matter of personal choice.

Regardless of size, each front lineman must be aggressive and have a strong desire to get to the quarterback before he releases the football. The front linemen must always keep the passer to their inside. Once the passer gets outside he can usually make good running yardage since the other defenders will be covering receivers downfield.

All pass defense special team members other than the front linemen must be selected for their ability to play pass defense once the passer has released the football. Linebackers and safety men will fall into this category. Although size is always good if the player has talent, these pass defenders should be selected on the basis of the following characteristics:

Quickness: The ability to move rapidly in any direction is essential in covering a good receiver with plenty of moves.

Good Hands: Once the football is in the air it belongs to the defense just as much as it does to the offense. The ability to catch the football is a prime characteristic.

Jumping Ability: Select pass defenders on their jumping ability rather than their physical height. Many 5'9" players can jump higher and obtain a greater jumping height range than some 6'1" players. (Test how high each linebacker and defensive safety can jump by taping small pieces of cardboard or wood containing measure heights to the goalpost, and let each defender jump, grabbing the highest measurement he can reach. Some players will be able to touch the crossbar of the goalpost, of course. See Figure 14-1.)

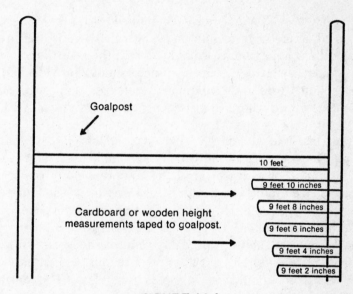

Goalpost

10 feet

9 feet 10 inches

9 feet 8 inches

Cardboard or wooden height measurements taped to goalpost.

9 feet 6 inches

9 feet 4 inches

9 feet 2 inches

FIGURE 14-1

Speed: Get as much speed on the pass defense special team as possible. Some receivers will try simply to outrun defenders rather than outmaneuver them.

The strategy of using the pass defense special team is simple. Anytime the defensive coach has good reason to suspect a pass rather than a run, he sends his pass defensive specialists into the game, replacing regular defenders. One particular example stands out in my mind. We once had a 6'1", 230-pound All-State inside linebacker. He was, of course, a tremendous player, but he did not have great speed. On definite passing downs we withdrew this player in favor of a 5'8", 135-pound kid. The small player wasn't a good enough ball carrier to be a starting offensive back. He wasn't quite good enough to make our first team defensive backfield. But he *did* have more speed and jumping ability than the 230-pound player. On passing downs the smaller player was all over the field, knocking down passes and making open field tackles that the larger player could not have made. His contribution to the team was invaluable.

DEFENSES THAT EMPHASIZE PASS DEFENSE

We do not feel that a defensive team needs to make wholesale defensive adjustments in technique every time there is the threat of a pass. Slight adjustments, combined with the insertion of pass defensive specialists in certain positions, should provide ample pass protection. Here are some popular defenses, along with suggestions concerning where to insert pass defensive specialists:

44 Stack: This defense lends itself to tremendous pass coverage potential. The presence of four linebackers and three safety men (see Figure 14-2) provides seven defenders available to cover the short flats, short middle areas, and three deep zones. The four-man rush should be adequate. However, any of the four linebackers can fire into the offensive backfield to put added pressure on the quarterback. With this defense it probably won't be necessary to send in as many pass defense specialists as with most defenses. The three safety men should be top pass defenders. The outside linebackers should be players with agility and enough talent to play pass defense. When using this defense take a good look at the inside linebackers and the front four linemen. Replace any inside linebackers who are not as good at playing pass defense as they are at stopping the run. Substitute defensive safety men make good replacements for these slower inside linebackers. Replace any front four men who might be big and strong, but who are not proficient at rushing the passer. Figure 14-3 shows these areas where pass defense specialists are most probably needed in the 44 Stack defense.

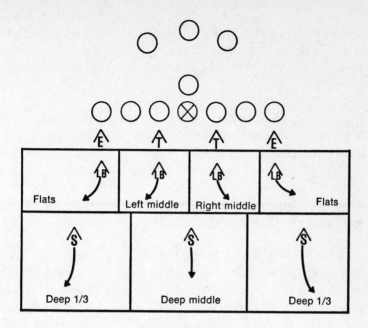

44 Stack defense

FIGURE 14-2

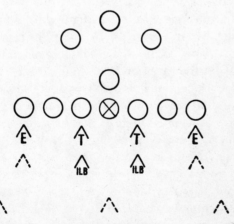

44 Stack defense.
Possible replacements needed at inside linebacker and front four positions.

FIGURE 14-3

4-3-4 Defense: This defense is a pro type defense that is geared to stop the pass (see Figure 14-4). It is also good against the run. The middle linebackers and front four defenders should be the only ones that might need replacing by pass defensive specialists (see Figure 14-5).

5-4 Defense: The 5-4 defense usually operates with a rotating secondary (see Figure 14-6). If the defensive coach chooses to stay with the 5-4 defense in obvious passing situations, he should give consideration to substituting pass defense specialists at the two inside linebacker positions as well as at any of the front five linemen positions. The outside linebackers and both safety men should be adequate. (See Figure 14-7.)

Wide Tackle 6-2 Defense and Split 6 Defense: Both of these six-man line defenses are very tough against the run. By using the defensive ends as well as the inside linebackers and safety men to protect against the forward pass, the 6-2 can be very effective. Figure 14-8 illustrates the wide tackle 6-2 defense and shows positions where pass defense specialists might need to replace regular defensive players. Figure 14-9 does the same for the split 6 defense.

5-3 Defense: This defense, utilizing three linebackers and three safety men, is a good pass defense alignment. Zone coverage is very simple, as shown in Figure 14-10. Consider replacing regulars with pass defense specialists at the three linebacker positions as well as at any front five position (see Figure 14-11).

Although we feel that it is good to stay with a team's basic defense as much as possible in passing situations (just changing personnel), there are some defenses that lend themselves easily to minor adjustments, creating a much stronger pass defense. **Example:** By replacing the middle guard in a 5-4 defense with a defensive back specialist, and placing this specialist not over the center's head but 10 yards deep, a very strong defense against the forward pass has been created (see Figure 14-12). By using a little imagination each coach should be able to make similar adjustments with his own style of defense.

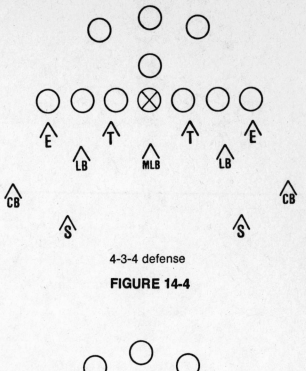

4-3-4 defense

FIGURE 14-4

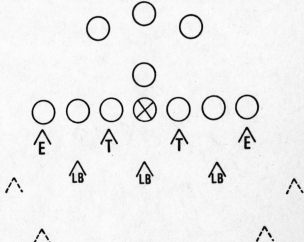

4-3-4 defense.
Possible replacements needed at front four and linebacker positions.

FIGURE 14-5

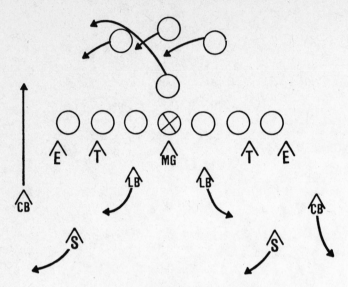

5-4 defense with rotating secondary.

FIGURE 14-6

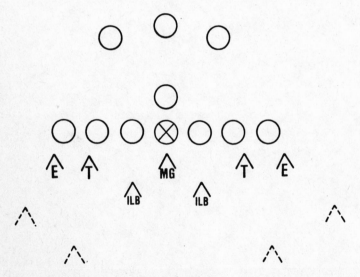

5-4 defense.
Possible replacements needed at front five and linebacker positions.

FIGURE 14-7

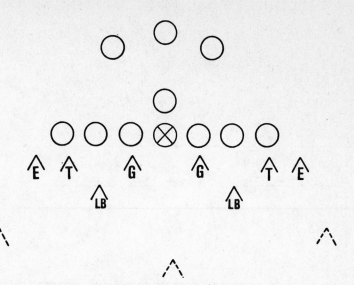

Wide tackle 6 defense.
Possible replacements needed on front line and at linebacker positions.

FIGURE 14-8

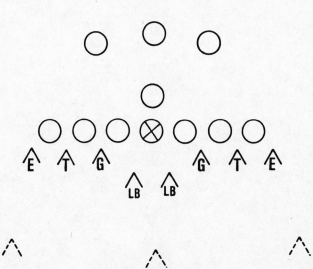

Split 6 defense.
Possible replacements needed on front line and at linebacker positions.

FIGURE 14-9

5-3 defense.
Zone coverage areas.

FIGURE 14-10

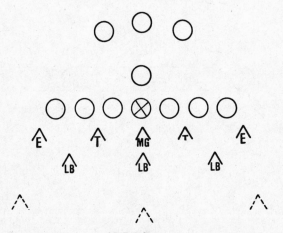

5-3 defense.
Possible replacements at front five and linebacker positions.

FIGURE 14-11

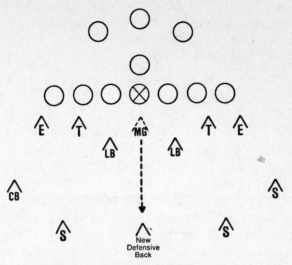

Remove middle guard . . . replace with defensive back . . . 5-4 defense.

FIGURE 14-12

PRACTICING THE PASS DEFENSE SPECIALTY TEAM

Practice for the pass defense specialty team should be in two parts: *group work* and *teamwork*.

Group Work: All front line defenders go with the defensive line coach and work on techniques in rushing the passer and keeping him inside. All linebackers and safety men go with the defensive backfield coach and work on individual pass coverage and catching the football. There are many drills for developing good defensive backs and linebackers, such as:

1. *Reaction drill.* Defensive players face coach, move right or left, forward or backward on his command. After several seconds of this the coach throws the football and the back catches it and returns it to the coach.
2. *Tip drill.* Two players execute the reaction drill described in #1. The coach tosses the football to one player, who tips it up in the air to the other player.
3. *One-on-one drill.* Line off an area about one-third the width of the field and about 40 yards long. Let a receiver

run any route he desires while the defender covers him. Defensive player tries for an interception or tries to knock the pass down. If the receiver catches the ball, the defender makes the tackle.

These are but a few of the drills that can be used to develop linebackers and safety men.

Teamwork: It is essential that the entire pass defense specialty team work as a unit as much as possible. Of course, they should get a great deal of work during the week preceding a game with a pass-oriented opponent. The drill shown in Figure 14-13 is excellent for the entire squad. Defensive linemen can work on rushing the passer. Defensive linebackers and backs can work on live one-on-one pass defense. Also the offensive linemen, receivers and quarterbacks can perfect their specialties. Of course, nothing takes the place of a regular defensive scrimmage against an 11 man offensive unit. Passes of the next opponent should be studied as to style and pattern. Use strong offensive personnel against the pass defense specialty team to create a true picture of the opponent. **Note:** Be sure to run the football occasionally to keep the defensive players alert to this possibility.

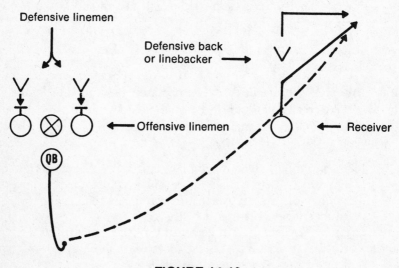

FIGURE 14-13

15

The Rushing Defense Special Team

WHY IT'S NECESSARY

Although most offensive football teams probably run the ball more than they throw it, it is the *threat of the pass* that forces defenses to spread their players over a wide area. Some defensive players must play in the trenches along the line of scrimmage while others must be stationed to cover the short pass areas and the deep pass areas. This allows the offensive line to have as many, and possibly more, players on the line of scrimmage to block than there are defenders on the line of scrimmage to control the run. Because of this we feel there is sufficient need for a *rushing defense special team*. The team would be inserted into the game in the following situations:

1. When playing against the offensive team that has proven in past games that it wants to *run* the football rather than pass.
2. When playing against an offensive team with a poor quarterback (passer).
3. When playing against an offensive team that has lost its quarterback (passer) through injury (either in this game or during the past weeks) and must rely on a young or inexperienced quarterback.
4. When the opposing team has extremely poor receivers or when good receivers are out of the game due to injury or some other reason.

5. When weather conditions (such as heavy rain) limit the chance of a successful passing attack.
6. When the opposition leads by a narrow margin and probably won't risk throwing an interception.
7. When your team is the underdog and you know you must stop their running attack to have any chance to win. Your game plan is to stop the run and gamble that their passing game is ineffective.
8. When your opponent is driving consistently on the ground against your normal defense and something must be done to stop them before they score. Although you may be vulnerable to the pass by using the rushing defense specialty team, you should at least be able to stop their ground attack and force the opposition to change their offensive plans.
9. When facing a team that has at least one outstanding running back. Unless you stop this back the opposition is likely to score several times. Make them change their game plan and force them to throw (which they probably don't want to do).

TYPES OF PLAYERS NEEDED

Normal defenses consist of several types of players. Some are valuable because of their large size (height and weight). These players are hard to move off the line of scrimmage. Many defenses will use from four to six of these players if they are available. Other players are selected for their hitting ability regardless of their size. Still other players (corner linebackers and safety men for example) may be chosen for their speed and ability to jump high to intercept passes (there may be three or four of these players on the regular defensive team).

However, this can be changed somewhat for the rushing defense special team. Since this team is primarily aimed at stopping the running game, more players must be brought nearer the line of scrimmage. The more defensive players near the line of scrimmage, the more difficult it is for the offensive line to block all of them. Therefore, more tough front linemen must be inserted into the lineup and several pass interception defensive backs removed. Here is a general plan to follow when selecting rushing defense special team players:

1. Get as much strength in the lineup as possible.

2. Get as much size in the lineup as possible. (**Note:** Here is one spot where the bigger, slower player can be used. Since he will be surrounded by a greater number of his fellow defensive players near the line of scrimmage, he can afford to be a little slower than normally desired.)
3. Get the best tacklers on the squad into the lineup.
4. Get the players who love to gang tackle for **they** will often have the opportunity to do so.
5. Select players who like to "challenge the offense," daring them to come their way.

When organizing the rushing defense special team, use this procedure:

1. Keep in the lineup any regular defensive players who have good size and strength and who are good tacklers.
2. Remove all but two (or in some cases three) defensive backs.
3. Replace the removed defensive backs with the squad's best remaining front line personnel (linebackers or front down linemen).

STYLES OF RUSHING DEFENSES

There are two different ways to build a defense that is strong against the rushing game. The *first way* is to continue to use the team's regular defense, but move the defenders (linebackers and safety men) up closer to the line of scrimmage. The *second way* is to develop a new and different defense designed through the imagination of the coaching staff. (**Note:** It is our belief that many coaches never use their own ideas in designing new and different defenses. Many take the attitude that "if this defense hasn't been used before it's probably not any good." I had the good fortune to design my own style of regular defense—the 44 Stack—and turn an 11-year losing program into a team that allowed only 17 points in a 10-game season to be scored on "this new defense." So it can be done.)

The first few diagrams that follow will show *regular defenses*, with linebackers and safety men moved close to the line of scrimmage, and several new rushing defensive specialists inserted into the lineup. Then we will illustrate several *"new" or "unusual" defenses* designed especally to stop a strong running attack.

Figure 15-1 illustrates the normal *5-4 defense* with two bigger, stronger front line defensive players inserted in place of the two pass defense corner linebackers. (Of course, we are only suggesting positions where bigger, stronger defensive players *might* be substituted for smaller pass defense backs. You must determine this according to your own personnel.) The corner linebackers have been moved to within 2½ yards of the line of scrimmage and about 2 yards outside a normally positioned offensive end. (Corner linebackers usually play 4 yards deep and 4 yards outside the offensive end.) The two safety men have moved to within 5 yards of the line of scrimmage instead of their normal 7 to 9 yards.

Figure 15-2 shows a *44 defense* with the four regular linebackers moved to the inside and the two outside safety men moved up just outside the defensive ends (about 4 yards off the line of scrimmage). Rushing defensive specialists may need to be in the lineup in place of the two outside linebackers and two outside safety men, all usually in the lineup for their pass defense skills.

A *6-1 defense*, sometimes called a 6-3, is shown in Figure 15-3. Make sure the two outside linebacker positions (see diagram) are manned by tough rushing defense specialists, and the defense should be solid against the run.

Figure 15-4 shows a *5-3 defense*. The two outside linebackers have been moved more towards the inside of the defense, and the defensive halfbacks moved up to within 4 or 5 yards of the line of scrimmage. The middle safety also moves up. He should be directly over the center and about 6 yards deep. Replace the outside linebackers and defensive halfbacks with stronger *rushing* defenders if necessary.

The *6-2 defense*, already strong against the run, can be strengthened by moving the two defensive halfbacks up to within 3 or 4 yards of the line of scrimmage. While playing to stop the run, many defensive teams still like to keep one safety man deep to try to prevent the possibility of a long gain should a back break loose. The 6-2 defense is shown in Figure 15-5. Consider possible replacements for the defensive halfbacks.

Some coaches like to play their regular *goal line* defenses all over the field if it is necessary that the strong running game be stopped. Figure 15-6 illustrates a *6-5 defense*, Figure 15-7 shows a *7-4 defense*, and Figure 15-8 shows a *Gap-8* alignment.

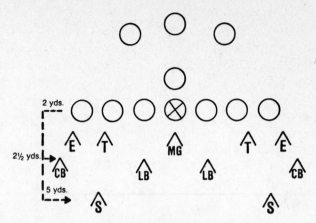

Tight 5-4 defense.
Consider replacing corner backs with bigger rushing defense specialists.

FIGURE 15-1

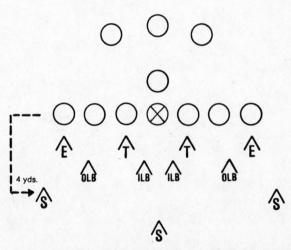

Tight 44 defense. Consider replacing outside linebackers and outside safety men with bigger rushing defense specialists.

FIGURE 15-2

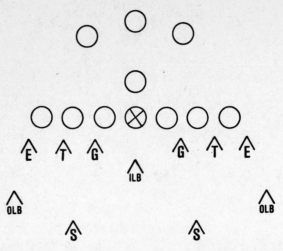

Tight 6-1 defense. Make sure outside linebacker positions
are handled by tough rushing defense specialists.

FIGURE 15-3

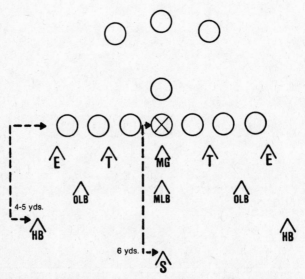

Tight 5-3 defense. Be sure rushing defense specialists
are at outside linebacker and defensive halfback positions.

FIGURE 15-4

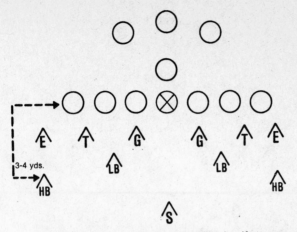

Tight 6-2 defense. Replace halfbacks, if necessary, with bigger stronger rushing defense specialists.

FIGURE 15-5

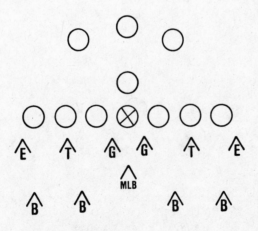

Goal line 6-5 defense.

FIGURE 15-6

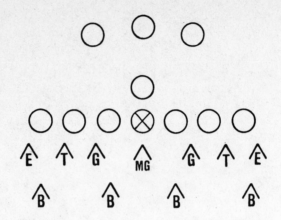

Goal line 7-4 defense.

FIGURE 15-7

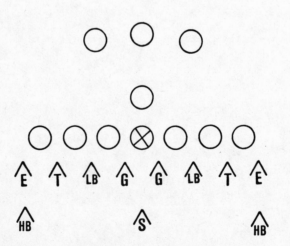

Gap-8 Goal line defense.
Strong rushing defense specialists could be used at halfback positions if desired.

FIGURE 15-8

Other than the conventional styles of defenses previously described, other rushing defenses can be designed. For example, when using a 44 defense a stronger rushing defense can be developed by making these changes:

1. Move the four linebackers 1 yard to their outside.
2. Remove the middle safety from the game.
3. Replace the middle safety with a strong rushing defense player. Station this player over center, about 2 yards off the line of scrimmage.
4. Move the defensive halfbacks up to within 5 yards of the line of scrimmage.
5. Replace any linebacker or halfback with stronger rushing defense players.

Now the 44 defense becomes a tight 4-5 alignment. It has good flexibility and is stronger against the run than the 44. Figure 15-9 shows the *4-5 defense*.

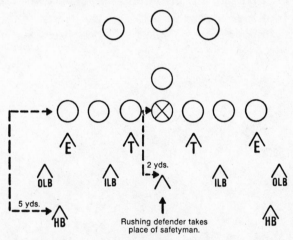

4-5 defense.
Possible replacements needed at outside linebacker and at halfback positions.

FIGURE 15-9

Figure 15-10 illustrates another unusual defense designed to stop the run. It is a 5-6 alignment. As there are no defensive backs 4 or 5 yards off the line of scrimmage, it is a greater risk than most rushing defenses.

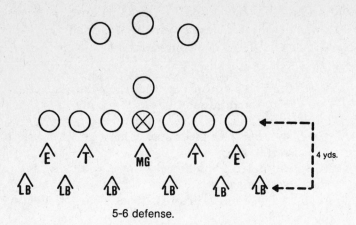

5-6 defense.

FIGURE 15-10

Figure 15-11 offers a five-man front, five linebackers, and one *rover*. The job of the rover is to line up in any area he feels the offense will try to run. One of the team's best defensive players should have this job.

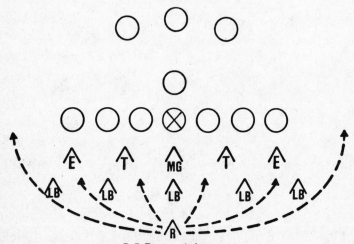

5-5 Rover defense.
Rover back can line up in area where he feels play will be run.

FIGURE 15-11

Although the defenses described in Figures 15-9, 15-10, and 15-11 seem strange, it is certainly true that defenses of these types can confuse an offense and at least make them change their game plans.

Special note: *When using the rushing defense special team we almost always use man-to-man pass defense.* The design of most rushing defenses does not allow defensive backs the luxury of sitting back and playing zone pass defense. We feel we must *challenge* the offense by playing tight, man-to-man defense against the pass.

PRECAUTIONS TO TAKE WITH THE RUSHING DEFENSE

While the rushing defense special team can be a tremendous asset to any team, the following precautions should be taken:

1. *Remain alert for the pass.* Although the rushing defense will be used mostly in non-passing situations, the offense might use the pass to try to offset any advantage held by the rushing defense.

2. *Get out of the rushing defense on second down and long yardage or third down and long yardage.* Just as the rushing defense special team is inserted into the game at any moment, it should also be removed as soon as it is not needed.

3. *Don't show the rushing defense special team until it is needed.* There is no need to allow future opponents to scout this team, and style of rushing defense, giving them time to prepare for it.

4. *Do not make changes in personnel* (when switching from the regular defense to the rushing defense) *just for the sake of making changes.* Consider the talents, competitiveness, and enthusiasm of each player before making wholesale changes.

5. *Although the rushing defense special team can be used anywhere on the field, consider the fact that it might not be needed when the offensive team is backed up inside its own 25-yard line.* The thinking here is to use the regular defense until the offensive team gets to the midfield area. The regular defense is a safer defense against long-yardage plays. There is also the possibility that an offensive fumble or penalty will stop their drive.

16

The Prevent Defense
Special Team

WHEN TO USE IT

The purpose of a prevent defense is to keep an opponent from scoring on a *long* run or pass play. The alignment of players on the prevent defense often allows short gains of 5 or 6 yards, but must never allow gains of over 15 yards on any one play. This is accomplished by moving a number of defenders back several yards deeper than they usually play and instructing them *never to let an offensive player, or the football, get behind them.*

The prevent defense should be used on two, and possibly three, occasions:

1. Use the prevent defense during the last two minutes (or less) of the first half in order to prevent a score by the opposition just before the first half ends. Use the prevent defense only if the offensive team is no closer than your 30-yard line. (Seldom if ever should a prevent defense be used inside your own 30-yard line. The exception would be if there was time for only one more play in the half and the defense had only to hold the offense from scoring for this one last play.)

2. Use the prevent defense during the final two minutes (or less) of the fourth quarter in order to prevent a late score by the offense that would give them the lead.

3. Consider using the prevent defense when the offense is

facing an *extremely* long yardage situation. Let's assume it's early in the first quarter. The quarterback has been thrown for a 9-yard loss attempting to pass. This play is followed by two 15-yard penalties against the offense on consecutive plays. The offense faces a third and 49 yards to go for a first-down situation. Unusual? Yes, but this type of situation will happen from time to time. It provides an opportunity to use the prevent defense. Short yardage may be gained, but rarely will the offense make enough yardage for the first down.

Of course, the prevent defense will not be needed in every game. But when it is used it can often mean the difference between victory and defeat.

PERSONNEL NEEDED TO PLAY IT

There is no place on the prevent defense for the big, slow defensive player. If used on the front line, he would be too slow to rush the passer or to pursue a wide play, or to react quickly to a screen play. And certainly no big, slow player could be used as a pass defender in the secondary. Therefore, when selecting players for this special team we look for front line players (there may be from three to six of these players) who have the *quickness* and *determination* to put a hard rush on the passer, plus a little *speed* to chase fast halfbacks. There is very little chance the offense will choose to run simple, straight-ahead, short-yardage handoffs in prevent defense situations. The offense needs large amounts of yardage. Time will not permit the "three yards and a cloud of dust" plays to be used. Therefore quickness and speed are more valuable assets than size or strength for front line players.

All linebackers and safety men (halfbacks) must have the same qualities—speed and quickness. These players must be the best pass defenders on the squad. They must know how to cover a receiver and react to the football when a pass is thrown. They must be disciplined never to let an offensive player get behind them. They must use their speed and quickness never to let any ball carrier or receiver get to the outside of the defense. They must be the team's best open-field tacklers and know how to make sideline tackles.

We like to envision our prevent defense as a gang tackling unit that converges on the ball carrier or pass receiver from all directions. On the high school level we find that 145- to 160-pound players who can move are excellent personnel choices.

DESIGNING THE PREVENT DEFENSE

There are four styles of prevent defenses that we have seen used effectively. We call them the *4-3-3-1* defense, the *5-3-2-1* defense, the *4-3-4* defense, and the *3-4-4* defense.

The 4-3-3-1 Defense: This is our personal choice of prevent defense. We like the one extra safety man placed behind all the other ten defenders. The 4-3-3-1 defense is shown in Figure 16-1. The defensive *ends* should line up head-on or on the outside shoulder of the offensive ends. They rush the passer from the outside. On a running play to their side the end is to turn the ball carrier upfield, never letting him get to the outside. The ends must always watch for the screen to the outside (playing the screen will be covered later). The defensive *tackles* line up head-on or on the outside shoulder of the offensive guards. They must rush the passer hard, but must be careful to watch also for the draw play up the middle.

The three *linebackers* are to cover the three short passing zones as shown in the diagram. They play zone defense until the football is thrown, then they go to the ball. The three *safety men* should be about 15 yards deep and play zone pass defense, as shown in the diagram. No offensive player should ever get behind any of these three players.

The *special safety man* lines up about 10 yards behind the deepest regular safety man (the middle safety). This player must be the most dependable defensive player on the prevent defense. He is the last defender between the offense and the goal line and must be a sure tackler. He must never come up towards the offense to try to break up a play quickly. His job is to stay deep, getting into the action *only* if the other ten defenders have been unable to make the tackle. As the run or pass play develops, this special safety should move laterally, always keeping himself between the football and the goal line.

The 5-3-2-1 Defense: This defense, which is a good prevent de-

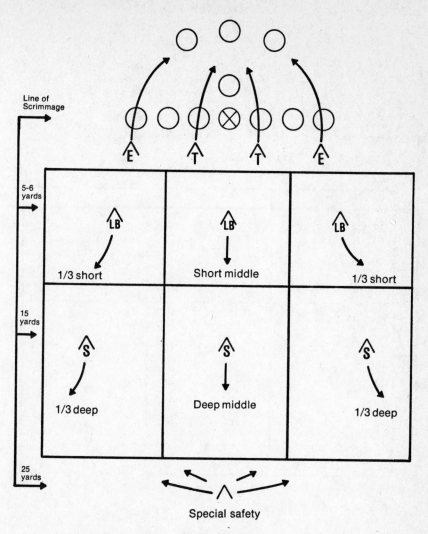

Line of
Scrimmage

5-6
yards

1/3 short   Short middle   1/3 short

15
yards

1/3 deep   Deep middle   1/3 deep

25
yards

Special safety

4-3-3-1 defense

FIGURE 16-1

fense for teams that prefer a five-man front at all times, is illus-
trated in Figure 16-2.

The defensive *ends* line up on the outside shoulder of the
offensive ends. They rush and contain from the outside. The defensive *tackles* line up on the outside shoulder of the offensive tackles.
The *middle guard* is head-on the offensive center and watches for
the draw play and the screen up the middle. The defensive ends
will take care of the screen to the outside.

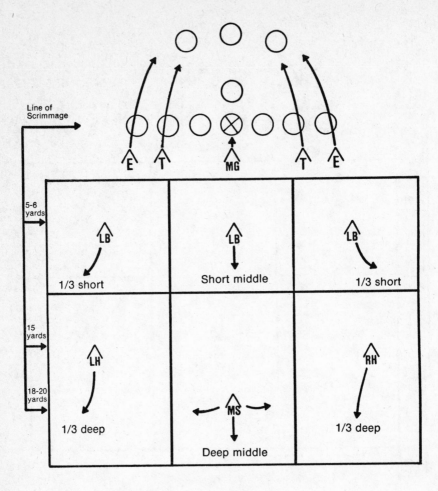

5-3-2-1 defense

FIGURE 16-2

The *three linebackers* move back 5 or 6 yards off the line of scrimmage and cover the three short pass defense zones. The *right* and *left halfbacks* drop back to 15 yards off the line of scrimmage and cover ⅓ of the field deep on their side. The *middle safety* is 18 to 20 yards deep and covers the middle deep zone, plus aiding the right and left halfbacks.

The 4-3-4 Defense: This prevent defense (see Figure 16-3) is similar to the 4-3-3-1 defense described earlier. The defensive *ends* and

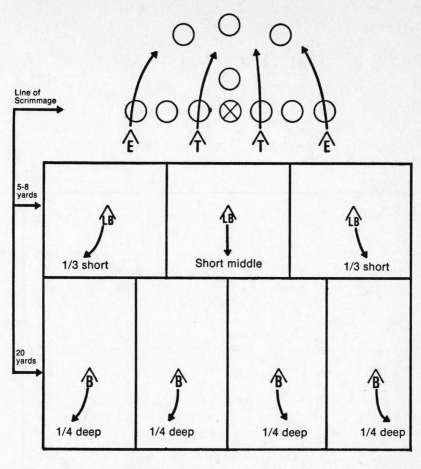

FIGURE 16-3

tackles play head-on or to the outside shoulder of the offensive ends and guards. They take outside rush on the passer, keeping him always to the inside. The defensive ends look for the screen while the tackles look for the draw play.

The *three linebackers* are 5 to 8 yards off the line of scrimmage and cover the three short passing zones. The difference between this defense and the 4-3-3-1 is in the *deep secondary*. As shown in Figure 16-3, the 4-3-4 defense places four backs side by side in the deep defensive secondary. Each of the four has one-fourth of the deep pass defense responsibility. Some coaches like this tight line of *four* defenders guarding the end zone more than the two previously described defenses that have a basic three deep pattern.

The last prevent defense will be similar in several ways to the 4-3-4 defense.

The 3-4-4 Defense: As shown in Figure 16-4, this defense uses only two defensive ends and a middle guard up front. The *ends* are head-on the offensive ends. They rush the passer or work to contain an end run. They remain conscious of the outside screen. The *middle guard* (head on the center) is responsible for the draw play.

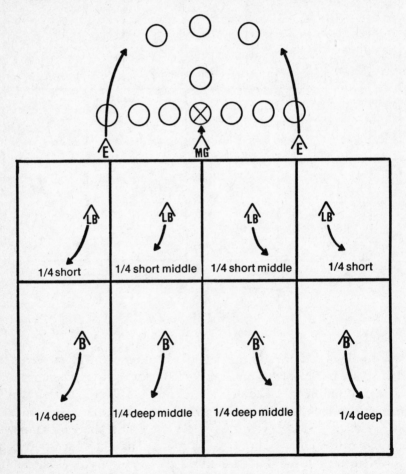

3-4-4 defense

FIGURE 16-4

The *four linebackers* are from 5 to 8 yards off the line of scrimmage and each one covers a fourth of the short passing zone. The *four deep backs* are about 20 yards deep and cover the four deep passing zones.

The 3-4-4 defense, to be totally effective, should have three players up front (ends and the middle guard) who are real battlers. These three must be aggressive, with a great desire to get into the backfield and cause some damage.

HOW TO PRACTICE IT

Since many offensive teams, in long-yardage situations, use a screen or draw play, the prevent team must spend considerable time practicing against these plays. Figure 16-5 shows a drill teaching the defensive end to recognize and cover an outside screen. Needed for the drill are two defensive ends, two offensive ends, two backs, a center and a quarterback. The quarterback takes the snap and fades to pass. Both offensive ends release on short pass routes. One of the backs blocks the defensive end on his side, while the other back is to block the defensive end for one count, then release to the side for a screen pass. When the defensive end on

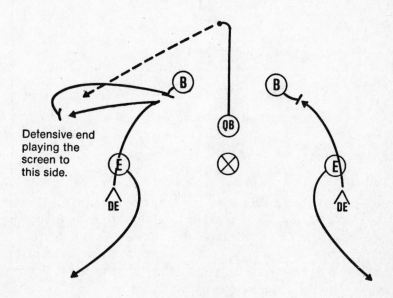

Defensive end playing the screen to this side.

FIGURE 16-5

that side feels the back release he should stop his pass rush and drop off with the back, covering him and preventing his catching the screen pass.

Figure 16-6 illustrates a drill for learning to recognize and prevent a successful draw play. Needed are two inside defenders, two offensive guards, a center, quarterback and fullback. After the snap the quarterback drops back as if to pass. He can continue to drop back to pass *or* he can hand off to the fullback who runs the draw play up the middle. (When running the draw remind the fullback to wait until the quarterback hands him the football before he starts up the middle.) The two defensive players resist being blocked to the outside and rush towards the quarterback. If the draw play has been called and the fullback gets the ball, the defenders make the tackle. If there is no draw play, the defenders continue their rush on the passer.

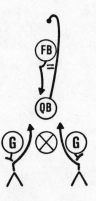

Two defenders checking the draw play.

FIGURE 16-6

To practice the entire team on the prevent defense, we line the defensive team in the desired prevent defense and instruct the full offensive team to run any type of wide open plays they choose. Screens, draws, reverses, halfback passes, long and short passes should be tried. Give the offense two, three or four downs to try to move a prescribed distance (perhaps 35 yards).

COACHING POINTS FOR THE PREVENT DEFENSE SPECIALTY TEAM

Here is a checklist of points to stress with members of the prevent defense:

1. Front line defenders must contain the passer and never let him fake a pass and run up the middle or to the outside.
2. Remember that long-yardage situations call for unusual plays such as screens, draws, reverses, etc. The defensive signal caller should remind all players in the huddle to watch for these particular plays.
3. Make safe, sure tackles. Never miss making a tackle by coming up too quick and hard and allowing a fast-stepping halfback to get away.
4. All defenders should try to make their tackles inbounds. This keeps the clock running. Often the offense will be out of time-outs and will try to get out-of-bounds on every play rather than being tackled inside the playing area.
5. The defensive ends, outside linebackers, and deep safety men should form a perimeter around the entire offense and never allow the football or a potential ball carrier or receiver to get outside this perimeter.
6. Safety men should never go for an interception unless they are reasonably sure they can make it. A tipped ball can fall into the hands of an offensive receiver.

17

The Two-Minute
Offense Team

WHEN TO USE IT

The purpose of a two-minute offense is to move the football down the field as rapidly as possible in order to get in position to score a touchdown or kick a field goal. There are only two occasions when it will be used: (1) late in the first half, and (2) late in the second half.

Because of its wide-open, go-for-broke style (which is often a dangerous brand of football), the two-minute offense will *not* be used at the end of *every* half or at the end of *every* fourth quarter. For example, the two-minute offense should *not* be used when the offensive team is nursing a tight 7-6 lead. On the contrary, the offense should be slowed in this situation. There is no need to use the two-minute offense when leading by a large score or when being soundly beaten. In general, the two-minute offense should be used only when the offensive team is tied or behind late in the half or at the end of the game.

TYPE OF PERSONNEL NEEDED

Almost any style of offensive formation (Pro-set, "I" formation, Power "I," Slot, Wing-T, Houston Veer, Wishbone) can be utilized with the two-minute offense. But some personnel changes might be needed for this special team.

As a rule, all players chosen for the two-minute offense special team should be the "game-breaker" type of player— that is, players who have a way of coming up with the big play, the long touchdown run, the unbelievable catch, or the great downfield block. All of these players may not be regular offensive starters.

Here is a position-by-position look at the types of players who should be chosen for the two-minute offense special team:

Quarterback. Should be one of team's best athletes, should be able to "make things happen" each time he touches the football; should be cool and confident, but at the same time daring enough to try something different if necessary to get the ball in the end zone.

Running backs. Should be best break-away threats on the squad; size is no factor here since offense will be more the wide-open style than the straight-ahead power style; need to be good open field runners, able to catch passes; should not be prone to fumbling.

Wide receivers. Having good hands is main requirement; ability to run with the football after catching it is necessary; must perfect sideline routes so that short "first down" passes can be thrown; need good faking ability and enough speed to go long.

Tight end. Should be a good blocker; needs also to be good short pass receiver with running ability after catching the ball; needs speed to run long patterns when called on to do so; must be good downfield blocker.

Tackles and guards. Besides regular blocking assignments should be team's best pass protection blockers; need ability to pull and lead wide plays or run quick traps, must be willing and able to block downfield (which is the real key to breaking the long gainer plays).

Center. Should be team's best snapper who can consistently deliver the football to the quarterback without a time-wasting fumble, should be a good pass blocker; should be experienced enough to block up-the-middle stunts by the defense and help protect the quarterback.

As mentioned earlier, the two-minute offense special team players may not be the regular offensive starters. For example, the team's regular tight end may be starting because of his size, strength and off-tackle hole-blocking ability. But the two-minute offense special team tight end may be a small player who has the ability to fake a block and slip behind the defensive secondary for a long pass.

And finally, make sure all two-minute offense special team players *can play under pressure*. Players who can't will draw penalties (off-sides, etc.) and will cause more harm than good. *Intelligent* players who realize the purpose and need for this special team, and who will be constantly aware of the clock and how far is needed for a touchdown, will aid this team tremendously.

COACHING THE TWO-MINUTE OFFENSE

Here are some valuable points to remember when coaching the two-minute offense:

1. Do not waste too much time calling long plays in the huddle. Develop and teach thoroughly a plan for rapid play calling. Examples:

Plan A. Have a prearranged series of plays to be used when executing the two-minute offense. Practice these plays in the same order all week. Do not huddle but carry out the plays as quickly as the team can assemble on the line of scrimmage. The prearranged play series could be in this order:

—Sweep to the right.
—Quick pass to left end.
—Sideline pass to the right.
—Draw to fullback.
—Long pass to wide receiver on left side.
(Start series again.)

Plan B. Call plays at the line of scrimmage with no huddle. Defense will not know what quarterback means even if they hear him since they are not familiar with his play numbers. Quarterback could call a "dead" play number followed by a "live" play number. Example:
Quarterback calls: "32. . .88." 32 is "dead" number. 88 means 88 Pass. Team runs 88 Pass.

Plan C. Huddle, but call next *three* plays to be run. Example:

> In huddle, quarterback says: "Screen left. . .22 Trap. . . .Divide pass right." Team runs these plays with no huddle in between. After these three, team huddles for next three plays.

2. Teach the offensive players to sprint out of the huddle faster than usual. Dragging out of the huddle eats up valuable time on the clock.

3. Use a quick snap count. Go on the "first sound" rather than using a long count such as "Down. . . set. . . hut. . . hut. . . hut" and going on the third "hut."

4. Use the sidelines. Develop short sideline passes or long down-and-out passes so that the receiver can catch the football and step out-of-bounds just before being tackled. This causes the clock to stop, saving valuable time. Ball carriers, on regular running plays, should be aware of the sideline and strive to get out-of-bounds just before being tackled.

5. If a substitute is to be sent in, he should start early enough to be on the field before huddle forms. Never waste important seconds making the huddle wait for a substitute.

6. If the quarterback is attempting to pass, finds no receiver, and has no place to run for good yardage, he should throw the football out-of-bounds. This will stop the clock and will often prevent the quarterback from being thrown for a loss.

7. Although the two-minute offense strives for long yardage plays, there are times where short power plays into the line are necessary in order to make a first down and keep possession of the football.

8. Make every effort to teach players to avoid making penalties during a two-minute offense drive. *One penalty can stop a drive.*

TYPES OF PLAYS TO AVOID

There is no way that anyone could make a list of plays and say, "Never use these plays during the two-minute offense." Because of different styles of offenses and differences in personnel, a play that would never be used by one team during its two-minute offense might be at the top of the list of another team. However, as a general rule, plays selected for the two-minute offense (with the exception of a few power plays to make short first-down yardage) should be plays designed to gain long yardage when successful. A play that consistently gains 4 yards, but rarely breaks for long yardage, is great for the regular offense, but this play has little value if the football is on your own 35-yard line with 45 seconds left on the clock.

THE TWO-MINUTE OFFENSE IN ACTION

Each team's two-minute offense will consist of different plays, depending on the strengths and weaknesses on the team. One team with a good passing quarterback will use the passing game, while another team will depend on its top running back to carry the two-minute offense load. Here is a hypothetical plan for the final one minute and 32 seconds of a game with the opposition leading 12-7. It demonstrates how a team might choose its plays to get into the end zone.

Down	Yds. to Go	Location of Ball	Time	Play	Results
1st	10	Own 45	1:32	Sideline pass to left end. See Figure 17-1.	+7. Clock stopped.
2nd	3	Opponent's 48	1:25	Sweep to right. See Figure 17-2.	+2. Clock. moving.
3rd	1	Opponent's 46	1:14	QB sneak. See Figure 17-3.	+2. 1st down. Clock stopped.
1st	10	Opponent's 44	1:10	Sprint-out pass w/motion by HB. See Figure 17-4.	+11. Clock stopped.
1st	10	Opponent's 33	00:59	Draw play. See Figure 17-5.	+3. Clock moving.
2nd	7	Opponent's 30	00:48	HB pass to Slot Back. See Figure 17-6.	Incomplete. Clock stopped.
3rd	7	Opponent's 30	00:41	Pass to back coming out of the backfield. See Figure 17-7.	+12. Clock stops.
1st	10	Opponent's 18	00:32	Quick pitch to right halfback. See Figure 17-8.	+6. Use last time out.

2nd	4	Opponent's 12	00:26	Short pass in flats. See Figure 17-9	+5. Out of bounds. Clock stops.
1st	goal to go	Opponent's 7	00:22	Sprint-out pass. See Figure 17-10.	No receiver open, no running area, ball thrown out of end zone to stop clock and not take loss.
2nd	goal to go	Opponent's 7	00:16	Fake run off tackle-pass to tight end. See Figure 17-11.	TOUCHDOWN!

Summary: The two-minute offense is certainly one phase of the game that demands plenty of practice. Work on it daily. (Remember, it takes only two minutes!) Use the stadium clock and a tough defense for realism.

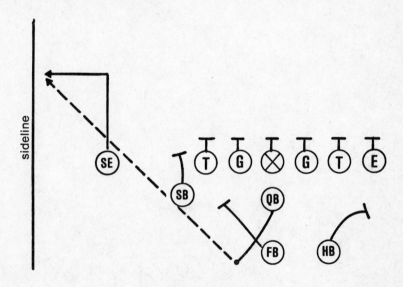

FIGURE 17-1

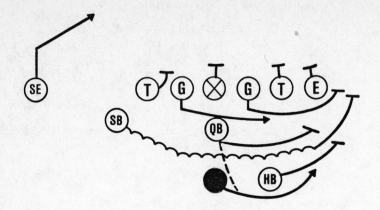

FIGURE 17-2

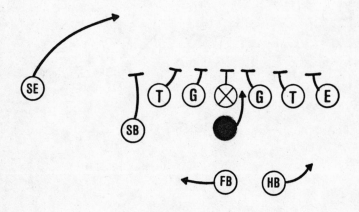

FIGURE 17-3

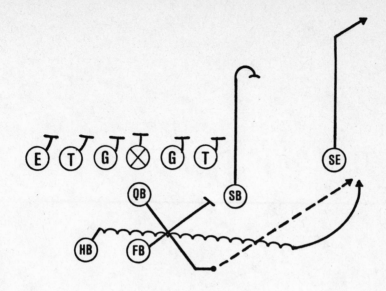

FIGURE 17-4

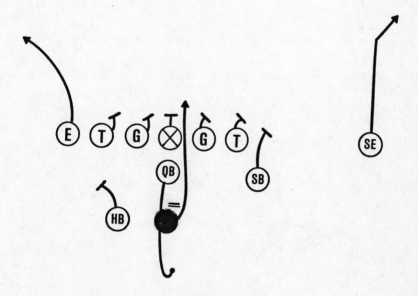

FIGURE 17-5

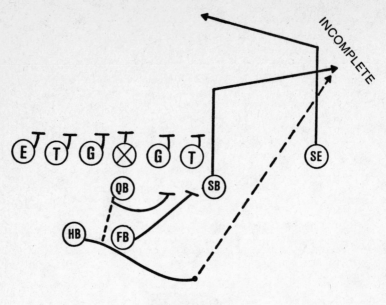

FIGURE 17-6

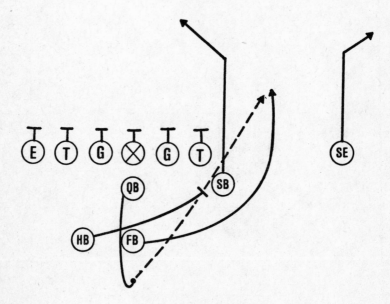

FIGURE 17-7

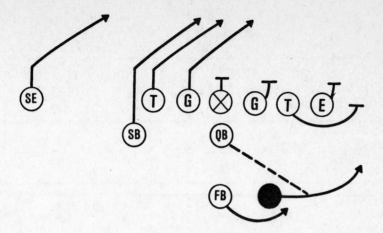

FIGURE 17-8

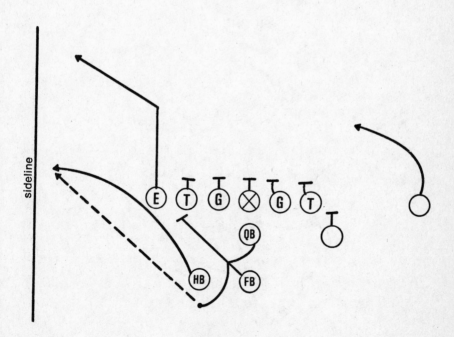

FIGURE 17-9

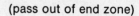

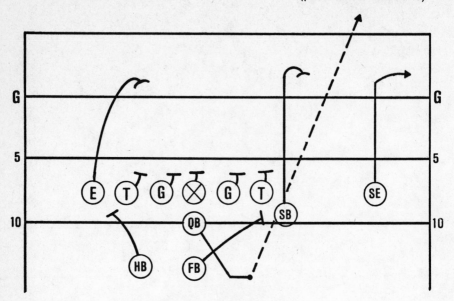

FIGURE 17-10

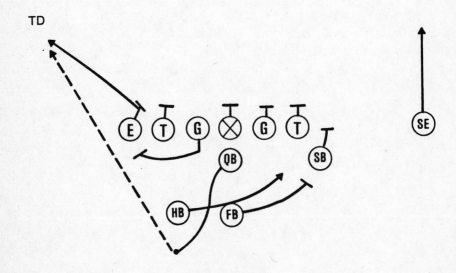

FIGURE 17-11

Index